All Things Made New

By:
Robert A. Russell

Printed in the United States of America

First Printing, 2022
ISBN 978-1-941489-63-5

www.RobertARussell.Org

Table of Contents

The Principle Of Metaphysics

The Key

When the Truth student is faced with a problem of life, he approaches it in the same way that the student of mathematics attacks his problem in mathematics. Knowing that the answer always precedes the problem and that it is given to those who believe (are steadfast), he applies the Principle, and the answer is revealed. X always is the unknown quantity, and it remains unknown until the Principle is intelligently applied.

The beginner in metaphysics, still working on the earth plane of time and change, often tries to find his answers and to meet his needs outside the Kingdom of Heaven through will power or human effort. Yet the clear demand of Jesus is "Seek ye first the Kingdom of God [Principle] and His righteousness [right use of the Law], and all these things shall be added unto you." That is, seek to know (understand) the Principle, and your understanding will make you free. It will make you free because Principle demonstrates Itself through your knowing, or understanding.

You may pray about the principle of mathematics, sing about it, preach about it, read about it, but these acts alone will never solve a problem in arithmetic any more thank talking of God will heal your body or fill your purse.

Pilate asked Jesus, "What is Truth?" But Jesus had previously stated, "I AM the Truth."

When you have money in the bank, you have principal in the bank. Increase (interest) then will be added automatically without effort on your part. So it is with your consciousness of God's Presence. When you KNOW that GOD IS ALL and that "The Kingdom of Heaven is at hand," you will have Principle in the possessive case. Then "All things shall be added unto you."

A problem in arithmetic remains unsolved only until the principle is known. The difficulty is not in the problem is known. The difficulty is not in the problem itself but in our lack of recognition and understanding of the principle involved. Both the problem and the answer are within our consciousness; are are dealing alone with our understanding of the principle of mathematics.

Now, if we think of the principle of metaphysics as applying to the problems of every day life, we see that it operates in the same way as the principle of mathematics. Jesus said: "Before they call, I will answer, and while they are yet speaking, I will give it unto them."

God (Principle) is the solution of every problem, the fulfillment of every need, and the answer to every question; the fulfillment or answer (like the solution in mathematics) is inherent in the consciousness. All we need to do is bring out the Good already in manifestation and to harmonize our minds with His mind.

For many, this idea will be a departure in spiritual practice. It means simply that every man answers his own prayers. Jesus said, "It is done unto you according to your belief." If you believe that the Kingdom of Heaven is at hand, *Now,* and believe, too, that you are in it and it is in you, the answer (already established) will come. If you do not believe, the answer will be delayed. To believe that God answers prayers only because we pray is to believe that the universe is a minus quantity, incomplete, unfinished, and unknown.

The great difference, then, between the orthodox conception of God's response and the metaphysical conception is the tense. The three-dimensional (human) mind works on the assumption that God is in the process of becoming or doing something, that He must be cajoled, entreated, begged, beseeched, placated, and implored to do certain things; the four-dimensional (Absolute) Mind works on the premise that "It is done." Jesus did not beg God to supply His Needs, to heal the sick, to feed the hungry, or to raise the dead. He always approached Him with the absolute conviction that "It is done." We too must know that the answer is here. The need is fulfilled. The problem is solved. The sick are healed. The hungry are fed. GOD IS. Heaven is at hand. All things are now ready. Every thing we need, desire, hope, or pray for IS at this moment. Apply the Principle, and we get results. Ignore the Principle, and we get delay. But always the imperious command is, "Seek ye first the Principle [understanding]." The Law on this point is just as exact as the law of mathematics; no evasion or side-stepping is permitted. IF GOD IS ALL, there cannot be God and something else.

"PROVE ME NOW HEREWITH SAITH THE LORD OF HOSTS." What God demands of us is proof and not praise, acknowledgement and not begging, intelligent cooperation and not wishful thinking. "Be not deceived, God is not mocked; for whatsoever a man soweth that shall he also reap." In other words, you take out of your prayer exactly what you put into it. When Jesus said, "The Kingdom of

Heaven is at hand," it was just as though He had said, "There is no sickness, poverty, evil or limitation of any kind except in man's thought of belief." How could there be limitation or evil in Heaven? Since man is sick, limited, and impoverished only in belief, he can be healed only in belief.

Part One
Nine Charts Depicting The Results of Primal Errors and The Way to Correct Them.

Fear

Anger

Criticism

Jealousy

Negativism

Worry

Self-Centeredness

Inferiority

Resentment

Fear—Faith In Evil

WHAT IT DOES

Fear lays the foundation for all kinds of disease and gives power to every enemy.

It produces more serious physical ailments than any other one emotion.

It slows down the circulation, changes the secretions, and wastes energy.

It causes loss of appetite, jaded nerves, depletion, debility, incapacity, and helplessness.

It paralyzes effort and cripples ambition, enthusiasm, and self-confidence. It brings premature old age. It is slow suicide.

It suppresses, depresses, and strangles. It benumbs initiative and makes the mind non-productive.

"By fearing an evil we give it power over us—it has no power of its own, only that which is bestowed upon it. It would have

Don't be so serious; learn to laugh at yourself.

Do not give power to what others think or say about you.

Do not think of your troubles at nigh when you retire.

Self-Centeredness
Living Against Yourself

SOUL-MIND — SPIRIT

MAN

BODY

WHAT IT DOES

The self-centered person is circumstance-directed, self-disrupted, self-isolated, self-frustrated, and self-defeated. Close to the better things of life, he suffers from self-pity, aberrations, sadness, disillusionment, loneliness, and disease.

He whose mind is turned in upon itself develops chemical changes in his body which manifest as weakness and decay. His system becomes subnormal or abnormal.

The self-centered mind is both cramped and sluggish. Such a mind interferes with the normal functions of the body, producing a stagnant and dormant condition; its action is to contract the cells into a state of inactivity.

Self-centeredness is one of the chief causes of poor circulation, costiveness, and surliness.

The self-centered are the disappointed, troubled, uncertain, fearful, sour, cantankerous, critical, vengeful, tired, undecided, discouraged, upset, unhealthy, unsuccessful, hopeless, mediocre, unpleasant, unhappy people of the world.

God-Centeredness

SOUL-MIND
SPIRIT
MAN
BODY

CORRECTION

The only antidote for egocentricity is Godcentricity—the surrendering of the smaller self so that the greater self may live. "It is no longer I that live, but Christ liveth in me," said Paul.

The egocentric must look away from self to God; he must stop thinking about self and think in terms beyond self. He must be other-regarding; he must lose himself in others.

Since self-centeredness is the cause of all human troubles, they can be dissipated only by the change to God-consciousness.

Just as self-centeredness slows down, scatters and divides the forces of the body, so God-centeredness speeds them up, equalizes them and causes them to work together in perfect harmony.

To overcome self-centeredness, make everything in your life serve God. Own all things, but let nothing own you; recognize that nothing is yours until you share it with others.

Learn to live without self-reference, self-importance, self-possession, and self-regard. Stop using the terms "my" and "mine"; do everything to the glory of God. "The Father within, He doeth the works."

Do not try to impress others with what you know, have, or do.

You accomplish most when you are "thinking about something other than self. Be so close to God in thought that when people think of you, they think of God."

Inferiority
Living Against One's Best Interests

WHAT IT DOES

A *complex,* according to the dictionary, is "a group of ideas of spontaneous and emotional character associated by the individual with a particular subject often indicating a kind of mental abnormality arising from repressed instincts or the like." Thus, an inferiority complex would be a group of limited, restricting, and inhibiting ideas associated with the self until they are embodied in one's life.

An inferiority complex is a black of understanding and faith in one's self. It is squandering God's possibilities; it results from living in the part instead of the whole. The inferior personality is comparable to an eight-cylinder automobile running on one cylinder. Bounded on four sides by himself, he has shut himself off from life.

Inferiority finds escape usually by false fronts, artificiality, superficiality, delusions of grandeur, boasting, and swaggering; in slamming doors, pacing the floor, stomping the foot, and finding fault; in argument, in negative moods, sulkiness, temper, and childish behavior; in shouting, in discrediting others, and in make-believe and pretense.

The inferiority complex turns giants into dwarfs, makes valuable men cheap, strong men weak, brilliant men dull, useful men useless, aggressive men retiring, positive men negative, and prosperous men poor.

Larger Consciousness of Yourself

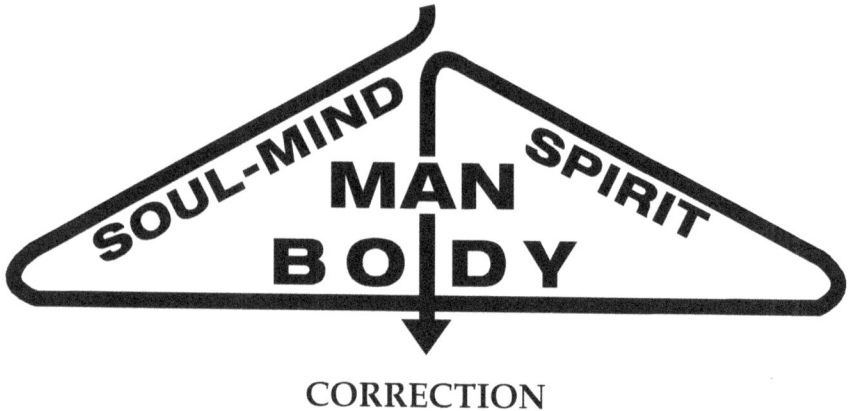

CORRECTION

In overcoming an inferiority complex, stand absolutely upon your own center, make your own decisions at all times, refuse to let others think for you, and keep water-tight compartments in your life where no one is allowed, to intrude.

See and think of yourself as you are in God; get the proper balance between yourself and other people. Know that you are important to the world and that there is a niche in it which only you can fill. Live and work, not for the approval of man, but for the approval of God.

Never think or speak of your limitations or deficiencies and never ascribe power to any but God. Never "look up" to others and never put them or their accomplishments above your own possibilities. Never lose sight of the greater man God intended you to be. Never react positively to negative things. Never fight your limitations; dedicate them instead.

Never depreciate yourself in any way; never speak meanly of yourself. Always at all times and under all circumstances, "feel" your importance in Cluist and know that destiny is centered in you. Do not tell all you now and do not apologize, or explain, or give reasons for what you do. Since God is the same in all men, you are equal to all men.

Resentment
Living Against Others

WHAT IT DOES

An undedicated resentment festers in the mind and heart like a boil in the body. It disturbs the emotions, develops complexes, produces allergies, dampens enthusiasm, destroys perspective, paralyzes nerve fibres, kills endeavor, mortgages the future, drains energy, blasts hopes, decentralizes aims, and leaves the victim barren, stricken, shattered, thwarted, empty and despairing.

It is one of the chief sources of self-pity, conflict, revenge, bitterness, oversensitivity, indigestion, prejudice, inharmony, anxiety, envy, jealousy, hatred, and selfishness. The resentful person is never at peace and never happy. He is always haunted, uncertain, and dogged by the shadows which his resentments cast across his path. He gains nothing from carrying these mental weights but lost vitality, stooped shoulders, blighted ideals, destroyed hopes, wrinkles and a short life.

There are many reasons why no one can afford to be resentful toward another. Chief among them is the adverse effect which resentment has upon all of one's social relationships. When you allow another to make you resentful, you are giving that person power over you. You are weakening yourself. When you try to punish or "get even" with him, you are making an enemy of yourself.

Love And Forgiveness

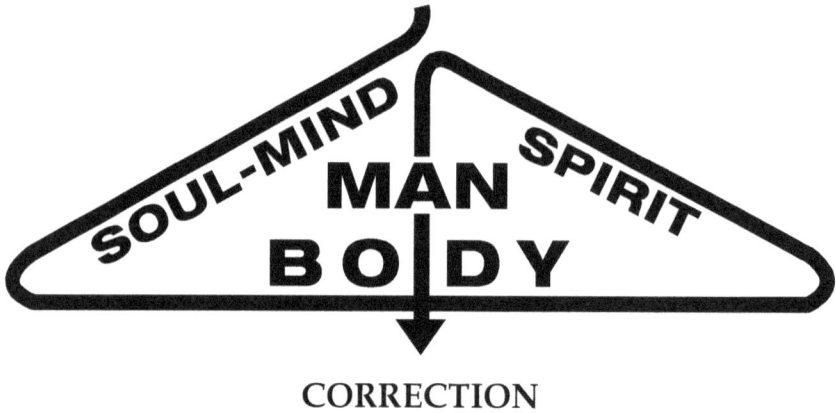

CORRECTION

Exercising love, agreement, self-mastery, and self-control is the most effective way of removing resentment. When we understand that there is only One Self, we shall see that in resenting others we are resenting ourselves.

Jesus said, "Love your enemies. Bless those who persecute you." Why? Because it is the only perfect way in which resentment can be met. We are to love people, not for what they appear to be outwardly but for their innate goodness, for what they can become.

It is a sound rule never to see or speak of the faults of others, to forgive ourselves and others for everything at all times, to bring our resentments to the surface and face them honestly, to avoid suppression and repression; to cultivate good-will instead of ill-will; to agree only with the good in others; to blame no one for anything; and to refuse to be the enemy of any man.

Finally, let go everything in the mind that is antagonistic, critical, or resistant. When others would provoke you to resentment, forgive them in your mind, and forgive yourself for thinking resentment. Never prolong the life of an actual or fancied hurt or slight by feeding it with your thought. Never waste time looking for the cause of a wrong, and never try to fix the blame for anything. As Jesus said, "Let the dead bury their dead."

Part Two
Therapy

Profound Principles and Practical Techniques
For Solving Personal Problems

Substituting Self Consciousness
for God Consciousness.

NEW RESOLUTIONS

"Behold, I make all things new." Rev. 21:5

Since New Year's Day is the octave of Christmas, one of our most valuable resolutions might be to carry the spirit of Christmas through the entire year. If during the Christmas season, we have been a little more kindly, more helpful, more ready to see the good in people instead of the bad, let us resolve to carry this same spirit through the whole year. Let us hold the same kindly attitude toward others, the same feeling of good-will, and the same consciousness of sharing.

But maybe you are one of those persons who make resolutions every year and break them, and consequently you are skeptical of making more. Remember that you grow not by drifting but by deciding, and be bold enough to decide again today.

Prospectors hunting for gold staked their claims, and then went in with picks and shovels to work them. Today, we are going to stake our Christian claims for the New Year:

1. I will seek the Kingdome of God first this year and put Him foremost in my thought. I will take time each morning and evening for prayer, meditation, silence, and spiritual reading.
2. I will go to church every Sunday, unless providentially prevented; and I will go to Holy Communion once a week.
3. I will become a tither, giving one-tenth of my income to God, the church, and human need.

4. I will put others before myself this year, trying to be unselfish at home and absolutely honest in all business deals. I will rid myself of temper, self-will, pride, and hate.

5. I resolve to meet everything and everybody in the Christ-Spirit, to have no misunderstandings and no quarrels, and to take no offense at anything that may be said or done. If others say unkind things about me, I will realize that they cannot hurt me except through my own thoughts and feelings. I will look for the best in others instead of the worst. I will seek points of agreement instead of disagreement.

"I KNOW NOTHING BUT THE PRESENCE AND POWER OF GOD IN EVERY PERSON, PLACE, AND THINGS."

RING OUT THE OLD, RING IN THE NEW

"Put off the old man and put on the new which is Christ." EPH. 4:24

When we cease to believe in a "material world" and "material man," the *old* will disappear as completely as did the flat earth when Columbus discovered the earth to be a sphere.

The whole purpose of Metaphysical Science is to bridge the gap between the Spiritual world, which is perfect, and the material world, which seems to be imperfect. The world appears differently people because they view it through different eyes. Some see nothing but retrogression and decay; others see progression and growth.

The variation in experience is determined by the inner vision. If one's consciousness is true, the outer expression will be harmonious. If it is untrue, the outer expression will be discordant. That is why St. Paul told us to be transformed by the renewing of our minds.

How then shall we ring out the old and ring in the new? By keeping our minds concentrated upon the ideal world, and by keeping the Creative Power moving toward it. Many never rise in the scale of life because they are constantly changing their goals, plans, and desire. The result is that the Power within never has a change to help them complete anything they set out to do. It is imperative that we bring all the power of the mind into harmony with the object in view. We must hold the object before in view. We must hold the object before our mental vision until it has been thoroughly realized and established in consciousness. We must know that God has absolute dominion over our lives, our affairs, and our world, and that nothing of an adverse nature can have any power over us. No negative or destructive thought can touch us. No belief in sickness or limitation can dominate us. We are free because the spirit of health and plenty has absolute dominion over our bodies and affairs.

> IN CHRIST, I HAVE ABSOLUTE POWER AND DOMINION OVER EVERYTHING IN MY WORLD, BECAUSE GOD IN MY HAS ALL POWER AND AUTHORITY.

THE UNTRODDEN PATH

". . . ye have not passed this way heretofore. . . . Sanctify yourselves: for tomorrow the Lord will do wonders among you." JOSH. 3:4, 5

As we look back over the old year, there is bound to be a sense of dissatisfaction and disappointment with the way we have

43

lived it, the things we have done, the time we have wasted, the opportunities we have lost, the failures, blunders, and mistakes we have made.

Somehow the saying of the Apostle Paul, "All have sinned, and come short of the glory of God," take on new and personal meaning. In the words of the Prayer Book of the Episcopal Church, "We have done those things which we ought not to have done, and have left undone those things which we ought to have done."

Janus, the mythological God from whom the name *January* comes, was a two-faced God. One face looked into the past, and the other into the future.

We are told, as was Lot's wife, not to look back, but it is a good thing at the beginning of a new year to take stock of the old year. Where did we fail to measure up to the standards of Truth? How did we keep our resolutions of the previous year? How did we get the problems that came to us? What changes would we make if we had it to life all over again?

When you have the answers to these questions and have mentally corrected your mistakes, turn back again to the present, and determine to make the New Year the greatest and most perfect in your history. As Joshua says, "Sanctify yourselves." Search your heart and mind, and cast out all the limiting ideas and belief which have cluttered up your life. Let it be a time of re-dedication to the Principles of Truth, a renovating of your attitudes toward life, a renewing of your faith in God, and an absolute refusal to give power to evil or to allow anything to come between yourself and God.

The best guarantee of God's activity in the morrow is the consecration of the present to His cause. It makes no difference what the morrow may bring forth; if you are centered in God you will be prepared for anything that may come.

I PREPARE MYSELF TO MEET THE NEW YEAR AND ALL THAT IT CONTAINS, BY CONSECRATING MY HEART AND MIND TO GOD AND TO THE PRACTICE OF HIS ALMIGHTY TRUTH AS REVEALED TO ME BY JESUS CHRIST.

NEW LAMPS FOR OLD

"Cast away from you all transgressions, whereby ye have transgressed; and make you a new heart and a new spirit." EZEK. 18:31

"New lamps for old!" cried Aladdin in search of his lost, magic lamp. "New lives for old!" is the Christian cry.

Probably the most fascinating thing about the writers of the New Testament is their idea of death and new life. "They are constantly using death as a symbol of what a Christian leaves behind, and Life as a symbol of what Christ does in and for men." So St. Paul speaks of our discipleship as a "death" with Christ in order that we may also rise with Him into a new life. This resurrection is what God wants; that is the way He usually answers or prayers. We ask for health, or strength, or peace, or safety, or forgiveness, for those are the biggest things we know.

"But God wants us to have more than just minor repairs. He wants us to have nothing less than a new life in peace of the old. So He often answers our prayers by making us pray more and pray harder, until we come to see the new life, which is the real answer to our prayers, and often the only possible answer."

Many of us view the old year as did the poet, Louise F. Tarkington, who wrote:

"I wish there were some wonderful place,
In the land of beginning again;
Where all our mistakes, and all our heartaches,
And all our poor selfish grief
Could be dropped like a shabby old coat out the door
And never put on again."

In a very real sense, the New Year offers just such a wonderful place—a Land of Beginning Again. Today is a brand new unused day. There is nothing in it that can bind me to a repetition of any form of sickness or adversity in the past. It is going to be the best day I have ever known. It is filled with new opportunities, new possibilities, and new promises. Gone are the illusions, failures, disappointments, regrets, and mistakes of yesterday! Gone are the old beliefs, circumstances, and fears which have kept me in bondage to an unhappy past!

As I enter into the New Year, I shall live each day in the NOW. I shall break with all thought of the past, and I shall take a new hold of life in the present.

TODAY I BEGIN LIFE ANEW, LEAVING EVERY VESTIGE OF THE PAST BEHIND. NOW I AM REBORN.

EPIPHANY

"We have seen His star in the East, and are come to worship Him."
MATT. 2:2

"Epiphany" is a Greek word meaning *manifestation,* or *showing forth.* Just as Advent is the season of anticipation (preparing worthily to receive the Christ-Child), and Christmas is the season of realization (celebrating His birth), so Epiphany is the season of manifestation (showing forth the New Life which has been born in us). We have prepared ourselves for His coming. We have celebrated His birth, and now, twelve days later, we must transmute all the Light, Love, and Joy into practical action in our lives, bodies, and affairs.

The gospel narrative tells us that the three Kings returned to their country by another way. They did not go back to the old life of materiality, but agreed to resign their respective kingdoms and to devote themselves to the cause of Truth. They were so profoundly and permanently changed by their visit to the Christ-Child that the entire course of their lives was completely altered. They came to Bethlehem as rulers of material kingdoms; they returned as followers of Christ.

Our intention for today, then, is to follow the Star — not a star high up in the heavens but a star within ourselves, the Light of Christ at the center of our being. Let us show it forth in our lives as confidence, wisdom, power, truth, strength, joy, and freedom. "Let your light so shine before men that they may see your good works." Let it shine in your world in the realization that God illumines you in all your thoughts, words, and acts. Let it shine forth in beautiful feelings, in purity of thought, and fixity of vision, in invincibility of purpose, in steadfastness, in kindness, and in love. So shall we transmute those gifts f the Wise Men into a higher and more spiritual level. So shall our "light break forth as the morning."

GOD IS THE LIGHT OF MY LIFE, AND I RADIATE LIGHT TO THE WORLD.

NEW FREEDOM

"Let us lay aside every weight – which doth so easily best us, and let us run with patience the race that is set before us." HEB. 12:1

When St. Paul thus admonished the Hebrews, he was talking, not about excessive clothing, heavy shoes, or a hundred-mile dash on the athletic field, but about heavy thoughts in the race of life. The "racer", of course, is a figure of speech. Each of us is a racer who must strip to the bare necessities. We must cast aside everything that will retard our progress, or slow down our speed. We must be light-hearted and mentally and physically free.

One reason why we fail to make greater progress in spiritual work is that we do not let go of the impediments which hold us back. We try to take up new things while the mind is filled with old things and there is no room left for new things. We try to put on a new state of consciousness while still clinging to the things that give heaviness to the old. We are held earthbound by our mental weighs and heavy thoughts. We crawl when we should walk; we creep when we should run.

When St. Paul really meant here by weights was the dull and heavy thoughts of inferiority, deficiency, and inability. He meant wrong attitudes towards life, toward others, toward ourselves, toward our work; the propensity to cling to old beliefs, old environments, old grudges, and old attachments. He meant thoughts of grief, limitation, self-accusation, animosity, criticism, failure, despair, and discouragement. All these thoughts are contrary to Truth; they congest and impede the flow of Divine Power.

These weights we lay aside by relaxing our minds and by letting God have His perfect way in us. Begin today, then, by realizing that you are free from everything that can impede your progress. Say to yourself many times:

I SEE YOU UNFETTERED AND UNBOUND! TRIUMPHANT! GLORIOUS! SPLENDID! I SEE YOUR STRONG! MIGHTY! FORCEFUL! POWERFUL! DIVINE!

NEW VISIONS

"He that hath a beautiful eye shall be blessed." Prov. 22.9

When Abraham moves into the Land of the Caanan, God said to him, "Lift up now thine eyes, and look from the place where thou art, northward and southward, and eastward and westward: for all the land which thou seest, to thee will I give it." The four directions are symbolical of the inexhaustible supply and unlimited blessings of God's love. Abraham could have as much as he could see, no more and no less. For us, too, the good is already established, but our experience of it is determined by our recognition, our faith, and our acceptance. We must "look up" from the conditions in which we find ourselves and see beyond our needs.

Now, ask yourself how much of Good you are seeing. Are you seeing the God-intended, perfect man you can be, or are you imaging the perishable and mortal man you seem to be? Are you expanding your vision by seeing and praising God for His Wholeness, or are you contracting it by seeing and magnifying your halfness? It is perfectly proper to ask God for things, but let us make sure that we ask for the right things. If the measure of our demonstration depends upon our capacity to see, let us ask for more vision, greater understanding, stronger faith, a wider acceptance, a larger outlook, and a deeper realization of the Good that is already at hand. The reason we favor the prayer of thanksgiving over the prayer of petitions is that thanksgiving recognizes the Good as already in our possession while petition admits our lack. If we see only the horizon of our needs, supply cannot come. It is always wise, therefore, to ask for spiritual gifts rather than for material things.

Let us endeavor today to get a greater sense of the priority and superiority of spiritual gifts, and to keep our eye single to Truth, our prayers positive to God, and our Spiritual Consciousness open to receive.

MY SUPPLY IS MADE MANIFEST BECAUSE MY VISION IS UPON GOD.

"IT IS LATER THAN YOU THINK."

"Boast not thyself of tomorrow; for thou knowest not what a day may bring forth." PROV. 27:1

"I know a land where the streets are paved.
With the things meant to achieve;
It is walled with the money we meant to have saved,
And the pleasures for which we grieved.
The kind words spoken, the promise broken,
And many a coveted boon
Are stowed away there, in that land somewhere —
The land of 'Pretty Soon'."

In an old forgotten garden in England is a sundial which carries this message: "It is later than you think." What a timely warning to those of us who are always putting off until tomorrow what should be done today! Procrastination is not only a thief of time but a waster of mental energy. It is one of the most prolific sources of remorse, regret, and disappointment. Putting things off is one of our greatest weaknesses; neglect is one of our greatest enemies.

Some day, like "pretty soon", never comes. It is a postponement of the blessings that can be realized and enjoyed only in the now. Belief is it is an admission of lack in the present and a handicap on the future. Someday — someday — thousands of somedays — always coming but never arriving. Yes "It is later than you think."

"Some day I am going to make my home more comfortable and attractive." "Some day I am going to give more time to my family." "Someday I am going to join the church." "Some day we are going to take a trip." "Some day I am going to do something nice for Bill or for Mary." How much richer life would be if we put into practice the things which we plan to do on some tomorrow! How many sad hearts would be brighter! How many failures would be turned into success! How many embarrassments and disappointments would be avoided!

When will we learn that right action in the present is the only guarantee of a future harvest, and realize that if we circumscribe the present with a thought of a lack, we limit the future also. The old song "There's a great day coming by and by" must give way to the quiet meditation:

I LIVE, ACHIEVE, GROW, LOVE, REJOICE, AND FULFILL MY DESTINY TODAY. THIS IS THE GREATEST DAY OF MY LIFE.

NEW CONDITIONS

"The former things have passed away – behold, all things become new." Rev. 21:5

Trying to change conditions is like trying to purify the water in the reservoir by painting the water pipes in your home. Jesus said, "Come apart from them and be ye separate." This is the first step in overcoming adverse circumstances — taking the power from them by taking away the attention. The second step is to change the cause of those conditions in the inner world by putting something better in its place. It makes no difference what you may do physically or mentally on the outside. As long as the "former things" (patterns) remain in your inner life, there will be unpleasant circumstances in your outer life.

Most people do not seem to understand that every thing in their outer world (both good and bad) has a counterpart in their inner world, and that the only way they can change their destinies and circumstances is by changing themselves.

It does no good to run away from an uncongenial environment because the uncongenial conditions are within ourselves. Being within us, they will manifest wherever we go. Jesus said, "Stand still and see," Do not hide or run away, but "stand still." Do not hide or run away, but "stand still." We do not have to handle the problems of disease, lack, criticism and failure, but we do have to turn off the "thought stream" that is feeding and sustaining them. When we shut off the flow of energy from the condition we do not like and turn it into one we do like, the saying, "Behold, all things become new" is fulfilled. The newness has come, not from any manipulation or human intervention but from the change in consciousness.

We have brought about new conditions in the outer world simply by changing the cause in the inner world.

NOTHING BUT GOOD CAN COME INTO MY LIFE BECAUSE GOD IS IN CHARGE.

A NEW SELF

"Neither circumcision nor uncircumcision availeth any thing, but a new creature." COL. 3:11

Remaking the self is at once the most difficult and most beneficial achievement in human life. It is difficult because it requires the utmost in self-discipline, and beneficial because it lifts one to his highest good. The average person if he is honest with himself will admit the need of improvement in his life, but he is unwilling to pay the price in sustained and intelligent mental effort to attain it. Man is perfectly willing to change almost anything or anybody in the world but himself. He is willing to be healed and prospered if—and this is the catch—someone else will do the mental and spiritual work for him. We forget, as Maeterlinck said, "that nothing befalls us that is not of the nature of ourselves."

But let us assume that you are different in this respect and you ARE willing to pay the price. What is your first step in crossing this gulf from self to God? The answer is: Be positive in your thought toward Good. There are only two kinds of thoughts, negative and positive; the most common of the negative thoughts is criticism of others.

"We like the story of Jesus and His disciples coming from across a very dead dog on one of their journeys. It smelled to the high heavens and disciples remarked very forcibly on the fact. But not Jesus. He went over to the dead animal, parted his lips with His staff, pointed out the fine set of teeth it had, and let go at that. His mind had no place for negative thought of criticism; only the positive thought of approval for whatever He could find to approve."

Let us take the first step toward the New Self by dedicating this day to seeing the praising the good in everybody and in everything. Instead of criticizing what is wrong, let us look for what is right.

THE GOOD I SEE IN OTHERS IS NOW BECOMING MANIFEST IN ME.

A NEW ALIGNMENT

"I of myself with the mind, indeed serve the law of God." ROM. 7:25

We have stressed the importance of positive thinking in remaking the self; today, we are to emphasize another necessity, controlled thinking.

Negative thoughts keep one in a state of discord and trouble, and uncontrolled thinking results in a condition of weakness and inferiority. Contrast the person whose memory is cluttered by "rehashed" conversations, yesterday's incidents, and happening that are as dead as Henry the Eighth, and the person who is tuned in to the Infinite, his mind fixed steadfastly upon his goal.

There is a cure for this unfortunate habit but it requires a capacity for patient work, self discipline, fixity of vision, and determined effort. If one has these qualities, there is no limit to what he can accomplish in self-development and self-improvement.

We know we cannot make this transition from limp-thinking to firm thinking in a day, or a month, but let us aim to make our thinking at least sixty per cent constructive within a year's period. We can accomplish this by balancing each negative in our minds with a corresponding positive, by offsetting each problem with a definite answer.

If we find that we have entered destructive and harmful thoughts in our personal ledger, we are going to balance the account with a set of positive thoughts. Further bookkeeping is simply a matter of holding the positive side in the ascendency. The metaphysician calls this process mental surgery; the Bible calls it burning up the chaff.

EVERY THOUGHT OF MY MIND IS NOW CENTERED IN GOD, AND I MEET MY GOOD WHEREVER I AM.

NEW GROWTH

"For he shall grow up before him as a tender plant, and as a root out of dry ground." Isa. 53:2

Longfellow was asked by an admiring friend how he kept so young and how he was able to write such beautiful poems. He pointed to a flowering apple tree in his garden and said, "That tree is very old, but I never saw prettier blossoms than those which it bears now. The tree grows a little new wood each year, and I suppose it is out of the new wood that these blossoms comes. Like the apple tree, I try to grow a little new wood each year."

Faculties that do not grow deteriorate. Muscles that are not exercised atrophy. Brain cells that are not used harden and dry up. Men who do not move forward are left behind. Religion that does not welcome new ideas weakens and dies. Consciousness that does not expand contracts. God never made anything in reverse. Retrogression and stagnation are contrary to the Law of Life. There is no turning back anywhere in the universe. Whatever God makes progress perpetually and everlastingly grows. His only directions are inward, outward, upward and onward. New life need new ideas. New life needs a higher consciousness. New Life needs greater visions. New life needs new ways of manifestation. Nature's motto is, grow or perish, rise or fall, sink or swim.

We shall think today, then, of the laws of growth. The towering oak tree is already within the acorn and the lily within the bulb. SO the God-intended Man is already planted deep within man's nature—the promise of what we can be. It is our duty, therefore, to keep interested in the things about us, to keep learning, and to keep growing. We must never be satisfied with ourselves or with things as they are, but must always aspire to new and better things. Let us put on new growth, then by loving everybody and every thing, and by centering ourselves in the ever-expanding and renewing Life of God.

MY GROWTH IS ASSURED BECAUSE MY MIND IS EVER REACHING OUT TOWARD GREATER AND BETTER THINGS.

A NEW OUTLOOK

"He that putteth his hand to the plough, and looketh back is not fit for the Kingdom of Heaven." LUKE 9:62

THE MAJORITY READ HISTORY; THE FEW MAKE IT.

There is a universal tendency among people to depreciate the present by glorifying the past. Old buildings are allowed to stand when they should be torn down. Old customs are kept alive when they should be allowed to die. Old methods of agriculture have caused famines. Old methods of water control have caused floods. Old methods of production have hampered industry. Old theories of education have kept people in ignorance. Old forms of government have made nations weak.

Whence comes this reverence for the past, this power which makes yesterday more important than today, this worship of has-beens? It comes from four sources: INERTIA (unwillingness to adventure and take risk—satisfaction with the old); CONVENTIONALITY (following the line of least resistance in order to avoid the opposition of others); EARLY TRAINING (voluntary acceptance of the thoughts and ways of others); TRADITION (the belief that the old is just as good if not better than the new).

Few persons realize how much their lives are influenced by the past until they break away from it. We sigh about the "old-time religion" and say it is good enough for us, but we forget that we are talking about a form of religion that is only seventy-five or a hundred years old.

Is there any reason why religion, customs, politics, or anything else should remain static in a world of change? Is there any reason why we should be Republicans, Democrats, Episcopalians or Presbyterians just because our parents were? Should we ride in covered wagons because our grandfathers did?

What has Jesus to say about this reverence for the past? To the backward look, He said, "Let the dead bury their dead." To the inert, He said, "Greater works than these shall ye do.

Let us change the course of our lives, then, by dropping old forms and traditional attitudes and by thinking for ourselves.

> I RELINQUISH ALL THOUGHT OF THE PAST IN ORDER TO ENJOY THE BLESSINGS OF THE PRESENT.

A NEW RELIANCE ON GOD

"Martha, Martha, thou art careful and troubled about many things."
LUKE 10:41

The story of Martha and Mary is a story about two states of consciousness—personal consciousness and spiritual consciousness. The one is occupied with the pressures and duties of the outside world; the other is concerned with the things of the Spirit. Martha was like a barometer, registering the hectic and frantic mind; Mary was like a compass, pointing always to the Truth.

We are prone to criticise Mary for not helping Martha in the kitchen sot hat she, too, could have spent some time with Jesus. But Martha would not have seen the advantage in such an opportunity while there were so many dishes to be washed and so much baking to be done. Mary would only have been in the way, a hindrance rather than a help.

How like Martha we arc! We put second things first, struggling wit the trivialities and small duties which clutter up our lives from morning till night. We spend time in the kitchen when we should be in the Upper Room before the Lord. We try to live by the material bread instead of the True Bread come down from Heaven.

Martha and Mary! Which shall it be? Work with strain or work with restful inspired labor? It makes no difference what our particular tasks may be, we can always perform them better when God works with us than we can alone. When we recognize this fact and learn to practice the Presence in our smallest or greatest needs, we shall eliminate all strain and static from our lives.

If, instead of trying to do things with our own wisdom and power, we would turn to God and say, "This is your work, Father,. Help me do it," everything would be accomplished easily and without stress or strain.

> "MY PRESENCE SHALL GO WITH THEE, AND I
> WILL GIVE THEE REST."

A NEW MOTTO

"Whatsoever thou shalt loose on earth shall be loosed in heaven."
MATT. 16:19

Seeking to solve riddle of life and to fortify himself against the whims of fate, an ancient king asked one of his courtiers to provide him with a maxim that would solve every human problem and meet every human need. The courtier meditated upon his commission for some time and then returned with the maxim: "THIS, TOO, SHALL PASS AWAY."

The inner meaning of this maxim was not at once clear to the troubled king, but the more he thought about it the clearer it became. Then he discovered the magic in the words, and the principle that gave them birth. He discovered that, by detaching himself from the things that did not matter and by relating himself to God, he could not only free himself from every human limitation but could hasten divine fulfillment in his affairs.

Five miracle words to change everything that may be wrong in your life! THIS, TOO, SHALL PASS AWAY. Grid yourself with their power. Embody them within your mind. Know that your mind receives them, believes them, accepts them, and acts upon them. Let them free you from every limitation in your world. THIS, TOO, SHALL PASS AWAY. There is no difficulty too great, no obstacle so strong, no obstruction so big that it cannot be dissipated by the power of these words.

Are you facing a crisis, fearful and worried? Then clear your mind quickly and make it receptive to the power of these words: THIS, TOO, SHALL PASS AWAY. Is it a thought of limitation or bondage that is troubling you? Then "loose him and let him go." Is it sickness that is laying its icy hand upon you? Then know that it is not of God, that only the Perfect and Good endure, that only the Real is True. Reflect your maxim in consciousness, and consciousness will be operated upon by it. "THIS, TOO, SHALL PASS AWAY" because God is greater than anything that may affront or affright you from within or without.

"THIS, TOO, SHALL PASS AWAY."

NEW ACTIVITY

"Hearken unto the statutes . . . that ye may live, and go in and possess the land." DEUT. 4:1

Our lesson for today has to do with Spiritual Law. WE are called, first, to the recognition that God is Law, and, second, to the realization that God's Law is the law of our life, the law of our health, prosperity, happiness, and well-being. Jesus did not say, "It is done unto you as you wish or hope," but "according to your belief." Call it what you will, God, Principle, or Law, there is but One Activity and that is Good. Know this. Accept it as the supreme law of your life, as the law of your highest good. Nothing can interfere with it; nothing can change it; nothing can neutralize it; nothing can shut it off. It is always operating. It is always becoming manifest as good or evil according to your belief. If you believe that God has a rival, and that evil is substantiated by a principle or law, then you will draw evil into your life as well as good. Conversely, if you know that evil has no foundations upon which to base its so-called presence and power, then you will draw only good.

When a man lets his mental level down, everything else in his life goes down with it. The organs of his body becomes sluggish, his faculties become dull, and his mind becomes confused; his affairs are upset, business gets bad, conditions become inharmonious, and everything is at a standstill. What is the remedy? He must neutralize his belief in inactivity by unifying himself with the Activity of God. The low places in a man's life can always be quickened into greater activity by harmonizing the mind with Divine Mind. If it is customers that he needs, he should daily treat himself for new activity and mentally see his establishment filled with people clamoring for his good. He should acknowledge God as the only Power operating in his life and know that this Power is bringing him only Good.

UNIFIED WITH THE CONSTANT ACTIVITY OF
SPIRIT, I ATTRACT ONLY GOOD INTO MY LIFE.

NEW VIBRATIONS

"I, if I be lifted up, will draw all men [manifestation] unto me."
JOHN 12:32

Thoughts of inability, inefficiency, inferiority, despair, discouragement, and depression lower the rate of vibration and bring disaster in the body and affairs; but thoughts of Truth, Love, faith, power, success, and confidence increase or raise the rete and result in harmony. One can go to the hospital and have growths and other manifestation of inharmonious thinking cut out of his body, but the saner and more sensible way is to bring the body back into harmony with God. Not everyone can do this, however, because not everyone has faith and consciousness of Reality sufficient to meet such conditions after they have developed. "Every plant [idea] which my heavenly Father hath not planted, shall be rooted up." It will be rooted up either by the Power of Truth or by the skill of the surgeon's knife.

In reality, there is no such thing as a human failure. There is only Mind, and the way IT is used. It makes no difference whether you are sick or well, poor or rich, your condition is proof that you have succeeded in the thing you believed in. You are just as much of a success in failure as you would be in success. You have simply compressed the Divine substance about you into the pattern you have held before your mind.

It behooves us to keep our vibrations high by keeping our thoughts in tune with God. That is why Jesus taught His disciples to pray, "Our Father which art in Heaven." If the body takes it tone from our prevailing and habitual states of mind, and if negative thoughts act like a break slowing down the rate of vibration and retarding the functioning of the organs, the way to restore the body to perfect harmony is to take off the brakes. In other words, we must remove all discordant thoughts from the mind and replace them with thoughts of an opposite character.

THE FREEING OF THE CHRIST WITHIN ME LIFTS ME ABOVE EVERY ADVERSE CIRCUMSTANCE AND CONDITION IN MY LIFE.

NEW KNOWLEDGE

"Ye shall know the Truth, and the Truth shall make you free." JOHN 8:32

There are two parts to our study for today — the foundation upon which all Truth rests, and the manner of demonstrating it. The first is contained in the Apostle John's words (I John 3:21): "Now are we the sons of God." The second is contained in Jesus' words to the woman of Samaria (John 4:24): "God is Spirit: and they that worship Him must worship Him in Spirit and in Truth." In today's text, Jesus sets forth both a condition and a promise. The condition is knowledge of the Truth (holding the ideal in mind) and the promise is freedom (objectification). "Ye shall know the truth," He says, "and the truth shall make you free." In other words, freedom comes through knowledge of Truth. When we know the Truth, we have actually come to the dividing of the waters. The old self leaves off and the new self begins. Evil dies, and good is born. It is fundamental to high achievement that we understand these truths and apply them to our daily problems and needs.

"Now are we the sons of God" has the same connotation as St. Paul's words: "Spirit beareth witness with our spirit that we are the children of God." Both mean not only that we, too, are spirit but that we are in the midst of perfection. NOW. Behind his body of seeming imperfection is the perfect body of Christ. Behind this world of discord and confusion is another world of peace and harmony. They intersphere each other, and we pass from the lower to the higher through our realization of our oneness with God.

The second great revelation is that the Truth being Spiritual can only be apprehended spiritually. The personal man must be still before the spiritual man can be revealed. The truth is that we are already free but do not know it. The Perfect Body and the Perfect Condition already exist. That which is to be IS NOW; it must be spoken into manifestation. "In the twinkling of an eye we shall all be changed." We shall be changed by the realization that Infinite Perfection exist here and now and that we are in It and that It is in us.

> THE FREEDOM OF CHRIST NOW ACTIVE IN MY MIND SETS ME FREE FROM ALL BONDAGE AND IMPERFECTION.

A NEW SET OF BOOKS

"And we also bear record; and ye know that our record is true." III JOHN 12

A very helpful practice among many Truth students is that of keeping a diary of their spiritual work. They do this, not because of a flair for statistics, but to have a record of their growth. They want to know at the end of a period what their growths or losses in consciousness are and whether they are succeeding or failing in prayer. As the businessman who does not keep a record of his affairs never knows his true status, so the Truth student who fails to record his demonstrations and failures is unsure of his balance.

If this sounds trivial, it is because you have never had the thrill and satisfaction that comes with such a practice. It is a good habit, not alone because it gives you a picture of your spiritual projects but because it furnishes an incentive for doing something better and bigger. It keeps you alert, expands your consciousness and your mind, quickens the faculties, increases the power of thought, and prevents your becoming lax in your mental and spiritual work.

Let us start this record today, then, and keep it true. Every time an intruding thought comes to you, remember that you have the answer. If a thought of lack or hard times comes, put it down in the first column; and then in the second column, put the answer: "THERE IS ABUNDANCE FOR ALL."

If you are upset about something, note it in the first column; then offset it in the opposite column with such words as these: "THE LOVE OF JESUS CHRIST IN ME DISSOLVES EVERY ADVERSE THOUGHT AND CONDITION, AND I AM AN OPEN CHANNEL FOR THE EXPRESSION OF DIVING LOVE.

Then drop the problem recorded, but repeat the answer until you impress it upon the subconscious mind. Declare: "THE ANSWER WILL COME." That moment, know that the good you seek is being given to you.

NEW MANAGEMENT

"And the government shall be upon His shoulder." ISAIAH 9:6

Success in living, like success in business is a matter of management is good, life will pay large dividends. If he management is bad, it will pass them. It is always important at the beginning of new period to check up on your manager (prevailing state of mind) to see if he is working for your best interests. If the records do not show improvement and profit, something is fundamentally wrong. You probably need a new executive.

We are recommending today that you look back over the last twelve months, take inventory, and determine whether or not you need a new manager for your life. If things have not done so well in business, if the children have gotten out of hand or employees have caused more than the usual amount of trouble, if there have been serious misunderstandings and inharmonies in the home, if business has been so bad that you are breaking under strain, then you need new methods and new management. You need a more efficient head to look after your affairs.

But where can you find such a manager? Right within yourself! You will find Him by knowing that the government of your life and affairs is upon His shoulder. Perhaps you have never thought of our text in this connection, but it has the same meaning as Jesus' words, "THY WILL BE DONE." Both ask that we do not give passive resignation to discordant conditions, but make open acknowledgement of the Activity and Perfection of the Divine Will and surrender self-management to Divine Management.

Let us relax then in the knowledge that our affairs are being handled by God. Let us relax knowing that God is in charge of our lives and that He is taking care of all our affairs. Let us live in the realization that He is now taking over every responsibility in our lives.

GOD IS IN CHARGE OF MY LIFE AND AFFAIRS,
AND I AM BLESSED WITH ABUNDANT SUPPLY.

A NEW OPENING

"Behold, I stand at the door, and knock; if any man hear my voice, and open the door, I will come in to him, and will sup with him, and be with me." REV. 3:20

Before one can find new openings in the world, he must first find new openings within his mind. He must open the door of his consciousness so that the good he is seeking can enter his life. When Jesus said "If any man . . . open the door," He was talking about the door into a man's consciousness. He was talking about agreement, acceptance, and receptivity. Acceptance is not a passive attitude of wishing or hoping for the good things but a positive attitude toward them, a dynamic faith calling forth that which is inherently good in everybody and every thing. Resistance closes the door; acceptance opens it.

"You remember Ohm's law in electricity, C=E÷R, C is the amount of electrical energy to be delivered at the point of use. E is the amount of available from the power house. R represents the resistance offered by all the things through which the current must flow.

"If there were no resistance, the full amount of current generated by E would be delivered. But there is always some resistance. Even the best conductor offers a little, and you can't deliver current without a conductor. So the amount actually delivered depends upon the power available, divided by the resistance."

"All that the Father hath is yours" as Jesus said, but it must come through you. It comes, not by hard work, struggle, or pain, but through receptivity, agreement, and acceptance.

These are the THREE KEYS which open the door to God's Treasure House. When you have them, you can get any good you desire. You can get this good when you eliminate from your mind all that offers resistance to it, all the non-conductors of fear, lack, worry, tension, hate, jealousy, and criticism.

Let us start today to change our discordant conditions into harmonious ones by blessing all the people, circumstances, conditions, and difficulties in our lives.

THE SPIRIT OF GOD NOW ACTIVE IN ME FREES
ME FROM ALL RESISTANCE TO MY GOOD.

A NEW DISPOSITION

"Be kindly affectioned one to another with brotherly love; in honor preferring one another." ROM. 12:10

A man's disposition is much like his mind. He can make it whatever he chooses. If it is bad, the desirable things of life pass him by; if it is good, they make a path to his door. But good or bad, a man's disposition is of his own making. Its quality is determined by his attitudes and reactions toward the situations in his life. A bad disposition is a decided handicap; a good one is a blessing. One drives away success; the other attracts it.

The ill-humored man is shunned, but he of good humor is welcomed. Therefore, keep your disposition in repair, especially if you are over forty.

One reason why so many older people are not sought after by employers nowadays is that they lack adjustability. They lack the ability of younger people to adjust because they allow their dispositions to get in the way. The years of experience of the older man should make him especially valuable. But a man who is unfriendly, resentful, suspicious, querulous, egotistical, tactless, stubborn, or fearful minimizes his worth and courts failure.

We have our choice of the kind of disposition we will have. We can be loving and kind in our relations with others, or we can be hateful and mean. We can be happy, responsive, forgiving, or reverse. The doing is in our own hands; we shall get from others what we give them. If we fight our environment, it will fight back. With love in our hearts, everything will improve; our bodies will be healthier, our work will be more successful, our relationships will be more peaceful.

Let us cultivate a new disposition, being ever sweeter, more loving, more forgiving, and more kindly.

> ALL THINGS WORK TOGETHER FOR GOOD IN MY LIFE, BECAUSE I AM LOVING, FORGIVING, AND KINDLY.

NEW EXPECTATIONS

"My soul, wait thou only upon God; for my expectation is from Him." Ps. 62:5

Before the metaphysician can help you meet your needs, he must know your thoughts about God and your expectation from Life. He must know whether you think thoughts that be little God, or thoughts that make it possible for Him to manifest Himself freely in you. He must know whether or not you are making room for the things you want by opening your mind to new ideas. When these points have been determined, he can map out a course of study, and practice that will change the whole trend of your life.

But you do not need a counselor to do this for you; you can do it for yourself. You can do it by analyzing and correcting your attitude toward the people, conditions, and things that you meet. Since God is Omnipotent (the only Presence and Power in anything and everybody), whatever you think about persons, circumstances, and things is in reality what you think about God. Your thoughts are the objectification of your own consciousness and your attitude toward life.

It is a salutary thing to go through your mind as well as your personal effects every so often and cast away the old and useless things that are cluttering up your life—old thoughts, beliefs, garments, and household things. Dispense with everything with which you are through. Make it possible for God to give you new and better things. If there is a need for some particular article, do not deny the omnipotence of God. Know that what He can do in the future for you, He can do now if there is a need.

Supply, like every other blessing, is a matter of expectation. Feeble expectations contract the expression of God; great expectations expand it.

ALL MY NEEDS ARE ABUNDANTLY SUPPLIED BECAUSE MY EXPECTATION IS FROM GOD.

A NEW IDENTITY

"Of mine own self I can do nothing; the Father within, He doeth the works." JOHN 14:10

The important thing in prayer is not the words, but the pray-er and the meaning, faith, devotion, and acceptance he puts into the words. When Jesus proclaimed, "Before Abraham was born, I am," He was not only talking about the tense of the Divine Response but of the precedence of the "I AM" in all spiritual manifestation. As Jesus became less and less prominent, the Christ in Him became more and more dominant.

We should be sure in making our affirmations that we identify the "I," or "Christ," with the words which we speak. If we think that it is we who make the affirmation or prayer, we are merely invoking the power of the human mind, and the results will necessarily be small. Such a prayer knocks at the door but does not open it. But if we think of the Christ in us as speaking the words, we are in the Center of Power and may expect large results. Jesus took no credit for anything that He did but always acknowledged the Christ (the Father Within).

Now, let us suppose that we are using the statement: "I AM the Lord that healeth thee." If we make this affirmation in the personal consciousness, the most we can expect from it is a little exertion on the part of the human self to make it real. There will be no concrete results from the prayer because we have no connection with the Power that creates. But if we realize when we make the affirmation that it is the Christ in us Who is doing the speaking, there will be an instant quickening of all the forces and functions in the body.

It is always good practice before making our affirmations to slow down the action of the human mind and to still the personal thoughts. And how shall we do this? By meditating quietly on some such Biblical quotation as this:

"BE STILL AND KNOW THAT I AM GOD."

A NEW ESTIMATE OF YOURSELF

"I and the Father are one." JOHN 10:30

Earlier teachers of spiritual Truth taught their pupils to fold their arms over their chests and say, "WONDERFUL, WONDERFUL, WONDERFUL ME." They did this not only to give the pupil a greater self respect but to awaken the divinity within him. The practice helped him to realize that as he held himself in mind so would he be held in the world.

The new theology does not picture a weak, inferior, degraded creature who has has incurred God's wrath, but a God in the making. It gives man a new respect for himself because it emphasizes the Christ or spiritual side of his nature instead of the human or "fallen" side. It gives new meaning and dignity to his life because it shows that he is more than flesh and blood, and bigger than the things that happen to him. If God is One, and if man is made in His image and likeness, man must be partaker of His Divine Life, Power, and other Attributes.

Emerson said, "That which shows God within me fortifies me. That which shows Him without me makes me a wart and a wen." The principal reason why more people do not reach the top in their chosen field of activity is because of their habit of denouncing, belittling, and depreciating themselves. They prate about their wretched memories and their inability to get things and to do things like other people. They tell others of their mistakes, weaknesses, ailments, and fears as if they were proud of their inferiorities and inhibitions.

Is it any wonder there are so many human door mats in the world? When will we learn that the world boosts the man who is up and kicks the man who is down, that it recognizes the man who believes in himself and ignores the man who belittles his powers?

Let us do something now about this ignoble trait. Let us get that "excuse me for living" attitude out of mind and lay claim to our unity with God. Let us know that we are truly wonderful. Let us realize that in Christ we are above the world and not subject to it.

> UNIFIED WITH GOD, I AM SUPERIOR TO EVERY CIRCUMSTANCE AND CONDITION IN MY WORLD.

NEW OPPORTUNITIES

He that is . . . "a doer of the work, this man shall be blessed in his deed." JAMES 1:25

He who believes that opportunity knocks but once lacks freshness and new interests. He is holding himself in bondage by an attitude that is antagonistic to his highest good. The Law of Life is that we attract circumstances and conditions which are in accord with our thought. Opportunities do not come because we seek them or want them but because we have made ourselves equal to them. The good things do not come by chance but because we have set the Law in motion by the power of our own thought. Consciously or unconsciously, we have provided a mental equivalent for them. If we make ourselves equal to the best, we shall meet the best.

How important it is, then, to keep the door of the mind closed to old, useless, crystallized thoughts and beliefs and open and receptive to new and better ones! If we keep ourselves centered in God, we shall always be receptive to new ideas and new viewpoints. We shall always be on the threshold of new opportunities, ready for new things, and aware of new gifts. We shall, as St. Paul said, "walk in newness of life."

RULES FOR ATTRACTING THE BEST

1. Put yourself in touch with the limitless supply of good things by knowing God as the only Presence and Power in your life.
2. Dismiss the thought that all the best things in your field have already been tried out and that all the remarkable things have been said, done, or invented. Rich fields in every line are everywhere waiting for the man who can place himself in the path of new opportunities.
3. Strive to make yourself equal to your ideal. Know that you are worthy of any opportunity the world can offer.
4. Keep your mind filled with new ideas, and new opportunities will seek you.

THE GOOD I SEEK IS NOW SEEKING ME. I GO FORTH TO MEET IT IN EVERY PERSON, PLACE, AND THING.

A NEW WORLD

"Be of good cheer; I have overcome the world." JOHN 16:33

Our world problem today is not alone political; it is also spiritual. It will not be solved by national sovereignty, international police forces, tariffs or economic controls, but by new spiritual bases. It has to do with the individual and his attitude toward God and his fellow man. Aristotle said, "The animal soul [human mind] being conscious of perishable things perishes with them." One does not accomplish anything by beating a dead lion nor by railing against the world. The way to change the world is to awaken to the Truth of Being, to see the world as it is and not as it appears.

If you do not like your world, you can change it by changing your relationship to it and by seeing it in a new light. You can change it be renewing, expanding, and perfecting your inner world of thought and by causing your consciousness to act always upon the limitless. Jesus did not overcome the world by changing the world but by changing Himself.

The real secret in building a new world is to build a new consciousness of it. If "retrogression is the one cause of bondage," then "progression is the only cause of freedom." We must not only fix in our minds a perfect picture of the things we wish to accomplish, and, as St. Paul said, "think on these things," but we must also live for them, work for them, and embody them.

As the Creative Power always acts upon our predominating thought, we must keep our thinking high, one-pointed, and clear. We must continue to build until the structure is complete.

THE SPIRIT OF NEWNESS IMPLANTED IN ME AT MY CREATION NOW COMES FORTH AS A NEW WORLD.

A NEW ADJUSTMENT

"But we all, with open face beholding as in a glass the glory of the Lord, are changed into the same image from glory to glory, even as by the Spirit of the Lord." II Cor. 3:18

Someone has said that the greatest synonym for intelligence is adjustment. If a man can adjust himself to new conditions as he finds them, he is in the ascending scale of life and moving toward his good. If he cannot adjust himself, he is in the descending sale and moving away from his good. Many churches still build their altars so that worshippers may face the east when they face the altar. Facing he east is an act of orientation, or overt adjustment to God. Since the East is the place of brightness and the source of the rising sun, it was believed by the ancients that any one who faced the Orient would be the recipient of special favors and blessings.

The word *orientation* means adjustment to first principles. The metaphysical student early learns the necessity of reorientating himself, of constantly changing his position in the law, or facing God for direction. "In a factory where mariner's compasses are made, before the needles are magnetized, they will lie in any position, but when once touched by the mighty magnet, once electrified by the mysterious power, they ever afterwards point only in one direction." Many a man loses out in life's race because he refuses to adjust himself to new conditions and will not let go of old viewpoints. By failing to reorientate himself, he loses many opportunities and blessings.

It is important at the beginning of a new day to get a fresh and firmer contact with God, to get His guidance for daily tasks and needs. Becoming orientated to Him, we not only become adjusted to any change in life, but we become masters of every situations.

THE SPIRIT OF WISDOM NOW ACTIVE IN ME HELPS ME IN ALL MY DECISIONS AND REVEALS THE COURSE I MUST TAKE.

LEARNING TO FORGET

"Leave off from your sins, and forget your iniquities, to meddle no more with them forever; so shall God lead you forth, and deliver you from all trouble." THE APOCRYPHA

Before one can really enter a new day and fill his life with new blessings, he must learn how to forget the sins, problems, and mistakes of yesterday. he must, as the Apocryphal writer says, "meddle no more with them forever." He must put them out of his mind so completely by putting something better in their place that they can no longer trouble him.

One of the principal causes of delayed healings and answers to prayer is failure to forget sins, hates, regrets, worries, and fears that caused he undesirable conditions. We are like the mythological two-faced god, Janus. We try to live and think in two directions at the same time. Physically we live in the present, but mentally we live in the sorrows and regrets of the past. Instead of magnifying the good, we remember the bad and deprive ourselves of the joys of the present.

Now read the text again, and you will see that God leads you forth and delivers you from trouble only when you cease to hold troublesome thoughts in your mind, only when you drop the sins of the past and cease to recall them. It makes no difference what the troublesome thought or unpleasant experience may be, God cannot remove it until you cease meddling with it, until you stop going back to it in your thought. The market is full of memory courses, but what we really need is a course that will teach us how and what to forget. Should you like such a course? Then substitute thoughts of god for thoughts of self. Instead of dwelling upon the mistakes of yesterday, fill your mind with thoughts of God. Instead of condemning yourself and accusing yourself, substitute thoughts of praise. You forget your iniquities by remembering God.

SINCE GOD IS THE ONLY PRESENCE AND POWER IN MY LIFE, I NO LONGER BELIEVE IN THE PRESENCE AND POWER OF EVIL.

TAKING A NEW HOLD ON LIFE TODAY

"Today is the day which the Lord hath made; we will rejoice and be glad in it." Ps. 118:24

1. I will live today as though it were my last on earth. I will crowd it so full of the good that there will be no room for the bad.
2. I will be joyous today, remembering, as Abraham Lincoln said, that "most folks are about as happy as they make up their minds to be." Happiness has nothing to do with externals; I will know that it is not a state of having but of being.
3. Today I will adjust everything in my life to God's Will and purpose. I place myself, my business, and all my affairs lovingly in His keeping.
4. Today I will take right care of my body. I will exercise it, nourish it, and carefully keep from abusing it so that it will be a perfect matching to do my bidding.
5. Today I will work to renew my mind. I will not be a mental drifter. I will keep my mind one-pointed and clear.
6. Today I will discipline myself in these ways: I will keep my mind off self and on God. I will do something kindly for some one, and keep it from being known. I will do two things that are right although they are disagreeable and distasteful to me.

7. Today I will hold a generous attitude toward others. I will be liberal with praise and will not criticize at all. I will find no fault with anybody or any thing nor will I try to regulate or reform others.

8. Today I will neither worry nor give external things power over me. I will not bring any adverse thought of yesterday into today.

9. Today I will have a plan and strive to do everything on time.

10. Today I will work in a calm, relaxed, unhurried, and peaceful state of mind. I will add perspective to my life by thinking of God as many times as I can.

WHO GETS FIRST HOLD?

"Blessed is the man that trusteth in the Lord, and whose hope the Lord is." JER. 17:7

The Rector stopped to chat with one of his young parishioners about the merits (and demerits) of the "Dodgers."

"Son, do you say your prayers morning and evening?

"Not me! I say them at night because I need God to take care of me. In the daytime, I can take care of myself," was the answer.

"That sounds fine," said the Rector with a smile, "but it's a bit dumb when you stop to think of it. After all, you don't get into much trouble when you're asleep. If you were only going to say prayers once each day, the best time would be in the morning when you are going out to fight the day's battle. But, of course, the sensible thing to do is to say prayers both morning and night. In the morning, they can be very short. Just kneel down and say 'Our Father' to show that you are a man and not just an animal—that you know and adore your Maker and want His help for the day."

"Yes," said the boy, "it makes sense all right. But I can never remember it."

"I knew one man," said the Rector, "who always put a book in his shoe when he went to bed. That reminded him to pray in the morning until he got the habit."

Few realize the value of morning prayer and the importance of giving God first claim upon their minds in order that He may be in touch with them before the world gets in. We speak of one day being better than another, but we forget that the success or failure of any given day is determined, not by luck, chance, personal effort, or outward circumstances, but by whether God or the world gets first hold upon our consciousness.

The blessings of God are new every morning; they are ready to greet you when you open your eyes and ready to attend you all through your working hours. They are prepared and shaped to fit your need, to strengthen, encourage, and uplift you, fulfill the Father's purpose in you. You become conscious of an receptive to these blessings by practicing the Presence of God, by giving Him first place in your mind, and by renewing your feeling of good-will toward others every morning.

SIMPLIFYING A COMPLICATED LIFE

"I will go before thee, and make the crooked places straight." Isaiah 45:2

The reason so many persons live miserably complicated lives is that they do not know how, or will not learn how, or will not try, to make them simple. There are twelve rules for simplifying living which will pay anyone to study, observe, and practice in his daily life:

1. Practice personal isolationism against the things that weigh, fret, or annoy you; always blame yourself, and not others, for the things that go wrong in your life.

2. Accept things as they are until you can make them better. Be yourself at all times and under all circumstances; forgive everybody for every thing.

3. Live each day as though it were the first one you had ever had and the last one you were ever going to see.

4. Never tell yourself or others how much you have to do, and never doubt your ability to do whatever your work is. Make things easy by doing them in the simplest way.

5. Give your whole self to what you are doing and never look for appreciation or praise from others. Do one thing and think about only one thing at a time. Take several periods each day to let your soul catch up with your body. Center your thought in God and practice complete relaxation as often as you can.

6. Since success and failure both lead to emotional disintegration, never accept either one as permanent. Both are attitudes toward life, and both exist only in the imagination.

7. Never take yourself too seriously. When your moods are down, know that they will soon be up. When you are depressed, know that it is only part of you that is depressed.

8. Acceptance criticism and opposition as you accept approbation and cooperation. Never try to please all of the people all of the time nor even part of the time. Go as far as you can to avoid a row. "It is far better to lose an argument than lose a friend."

9. Keep your thoughts and consciousness so high that petty, trivial things, and personalities cannot reach up to you. Never come down to error; never give power to evil.
10. Be sure your Center is right; never make excuses or try to defend yourself.
11. Build a large-sized cemetery in which to bury the faults and mistakes of others; never harp upon or dig up the past.
12. Keep your business to yourself; do not confide in others.

DISEASES THAT ARE CAUSED AND FED BY WORRY

"Banish all worries from your mind and keep your body free from pain." ECCLESIASTES 11:10 (Moffatt)

Chief among the diseases that are caused by worry and emotional unbalance are heart trouble, ulcers of the stomach, skin trouble, high blood pressure, rheumatism, colds, eye troubles, hyperthyroidism, asthenia, diabetes, and nervousness. Dr. Felix Cunha says that "the incidence of stomach ulcers goes up and down with the stock market." When the stock market is down, stomach ulcers go up. When the up, stomach ulcers go down. The reason is that worry generates an excessive amount of acid in the stomach; and where there is too much acid, like too much of anything else, there is always trouble.

The five steps in healing and protecting oneself against these dread diseases of civilization follow:

1. Do not carry so much in or on your mind. The people who are free from the diseases mentioned about are the detached, carefree, happy, irresponsible, unworrying drifters, tramps, and savages.

2. Learn to meet things and dispose of them as they come, or as St. Matthew says, "See and do not be alarmed." Walk up to your troubles as you would walk up to a scarecrow and pull out the straw. Look them straight in the eye, without fear.

3. Keep your mind occupied with the things you like and the things you like to do. Have an avocation; cultivate a hobby. Put yourself into what you are doing; take no thought of what remains undone. Relax while you work; get as much rest as you can, particularly after meals. The sleep you get in the hours before midnight does you twice as much good as that of later hours.

4. Learn to live by indirections (like an alligator), without wear and tear and waste of energy. The one sure way to heal the "sore spots" in consciousness (objects and causes of your worry) is by looking past them to God, by *out*looking and *over*looking them.

5. Furnish normal outlets for your emotions; express yourself from your heels. When you feel like laughing, laugh all over. When you feel like crying, cry all over.

HELPFUL HINTS FOR THE CHRONIC WORRIER

"So do not be troubled about tomorrow; tomorrow will take care of itself. The day's own trouble is quite enough for the day." MATT. 6:34

1. Nothing you worry about is half as bad as the worry itself.
   The person who faces trouble with worry must meet the problem at hand and all those which his distorted imagination and perverted sense of faith have built up. There is only one justifiable worry, and that is worry about worry.

2. Whatever gets into the mind and emotions gets into the man, and if allowed to remain there, takes possession of him.

   If worry gets your attention, it gets you, gets your mind, your body, your affairs, and your life. It is not only removes the controls from your life but closes the inlet and opens the outlet. The result is gradual deterioration and depletion of energy ending in mental and physical bankruptcy. Worry intensifies trouble and prolongs it. A worried mind is a tense mind. A worried mind is a closed mind. Worry contracts, while faith relaxes.

3. Worry never takes possession of an untroubled, quiet, and relaxed mind.

   "In quietness and in confidence shall be your strength." "Thou will keep him in perfect peace whose mind is stayed on Thee." "Quietness" here means to be detached, still, passive, and inactive toward the objects of our worries, and "confidence" means to be active toward God. In other words, we must "let go" and "let God." We must let go of our worries, troubles, and concerns, and let God handle them.

4. Live one day at a time; meet the present with the present.

   He who worries about the future meets his troubles twice, before and after they come. In a sense, the worrier is an atheist. He believes more in the power of misfortune than in the Power of God. Let go of worry, and worry will let go of you.

I CEASE TO WORRY. I KNOW THAT ALL MY AFFAIRS ARE IN THE KEEPING OF GOD, AND THAT ALL IS WELL.

THE LENTEN FAST

"If ye then be risen with Christ, seek those things which are above, where Christ sitteth on the right hand of God. Set your affections on thing above, not on things on the earth. For ye are dead, and your life is hid with Christ in God." COL. 3:2

The three primary purposes of the Lenten season are to condition us mentally, spiritually, and physically for a great spiritual awakening; to resurrect us out of imperfect states of consciousness into a realization of the more abundant Life of God; and to permit us to re-align ourselves with the Mind, Will, and Purposes of Jesus Christ. To this end, said Jesus, "all these things shall be added." We shall find greater happiness, health, supply, freedom, balance and peace of mind.

One of the best definitions of fasting is this: "Decide what you want most and concentrate on that." If you concentrate (center your attention) upon God, everything else will fall into its right place. You will deny yourself into its right place. You will deny yourself certain things, "renounce them", "drop them out", "give them up", "do without them", not because they are injurious, not because you do not like them or want them, but because you want God and Heaven more.

"Set your affection," said St. Paul, "on things which are close to Christ." In other words, "Decide what you want most, and let it be what Christ wants to give you." Do bad habits need correcting? Habits of thinking, judging, criticising, feeling, seeing, hearing, eating, speaking, or acting? Resolve to give them up, and to replace them by better ones. Reconsecrate your faculties, senses, emotions, eyes, ears, and tongue to the Truth. Bring your mind under control of the Christ Mind so that His Ideas may dominate your thinking and keep it in constructive channels. If you have been listening to animosity, gossip, and criticism, and "syndicating" them, discipline your ears and tongue to hear and say only that which is good, constructive, and true.

Now ask yourself what it is that you want most. (Is it freedom from fear, worry, jealousy, deceit, dishonesty, bad temper, selfishness, extravagance? Is it freedom from false appetite, overeating, overdrinking, oversmoking?) Then practice restraint through prayer and the surrender of your mind and body to God. Surrender them together. Pick out the worst things you can find in your nature and then "set your affection" on their opposites, or good qualities. See how quickly the lesser things will fall into place by falling out of your experience.

THROUGH THE SPIRIT OF TRUTH WITHIN ME,
I KNOW, SEE HEAR, AND SPEAK ONLY TRUTH.

GIVING POWER TO YOUR LIFE

"It is the spirit that quickeneth." JOHN 6:63

The secret of Jesus' great power and influence upon the world was the power of the Spirit that was in Him. He was Himself the embodiment of the Truth that "It is the spirit that giveth life." No pomp or show, no glittering robes or smoking incense pots supported him. No cathedrals or churches, no ecclesiastical or political activities, no ordinances, or disciplines, no universities or seminaries followed in his wake. Yet it is written that "Jesus returned in the power of the Spirit into Galilee" and again that "a fame went out concerning Him through all the region round about."

"Always wherever Jesus went," writes Allen W. Clark in one of his weekly letters, "men felt that there was something back of Him—some mighty power that they did not understand!" What was this power? It was a power born of a conscious and cooperative union with God.

Oh, I know we are tired and weary of hearing about post-war problems and responsibilities but the fact remains that we as individuals are going to have to meet them, not with the strength we natively possess but by opening our lives to greater power and reinforcement from within. As Archdeacon Neve said about present times, "the really important thing is to find what God can do through us, rather than what we can do for Him." Then how shall we meet the condition of being acted through and upon? By "absolute integrity of thought, speech, and feeling."

We can begin today by inviting into our lives the very Spirit of God, and by exercising the authority and power of that Spirit in our daily needs. "Where the Spirit of the Lord is, there is liberty"—liberty from uncertainty, insecurity, indecisiveness, and bondage of every kind. Do you have enemies in the form of anxieties, contentions, fears, hates, jealousies, and doubts? Then remember that they, too, are the children of God. Maybe you have never thought of your enemies in this light, but they are seeking God just as you are. They are seeking to be righted, or harmonized, with Truth. How are you going to meet their need? There are two ways: by repression or by love. In the first case, they are like "bad boys who, when put out of the class, begin to throw stones at the windows." In the second case, they are turned to higher expressions. The door is opened upward.

TURNING WITHIN, I FIND "A GREATER EXPRESSION OF THE CHRIST SPIRIT IN MY LIFE."

WHAT A PROMINENT PHYSICIAN SAYS ABOUT THE SILENCE

In Health Culture, a leading magazine, Rasmus Alsaker, M.D., the editor and one of America's outstanding physicians, says:

"When in doubt, go into the Silence and receive the answer you are seeking. Going into the Silence is to communicate within yourself. You forget the world and life's struggles and strife. You enter into your own holy of holies.

"When you communicate within yourself, you listen to the voice of confidence, the Voice of the Supreme Force that rules Life, and find the way to travel. When grief or worry appears, the majority are swayed by their emotions, and often do not realize until too late what mistakes they made when the emotions rule.

"The Silence is the quiet of one's own soul; it is where truth springs forth; it is where that inner illumination comes which enables us to see our own way ahead, and to light the way for others; it is the front of courage and inspiration.

"Within the Silence are all the great treasures with which man is endowed here on earth, and it is here that man can contact his Maker.

"So few go into the Silence! The majority do not know that it exists though they have read and heard about it. In the scriptures we learn that the loftiest religious geniuses of ancient times went to the Silence.

"Modern men and women should go into the Silence, now that the material world is so insecure. What do they profit by too frequent parties, playing cards or other games too often, or constant attendance at motion pictures, dances, clubs, and other amusements? They have no time to cultivate themselves; they have no time to relax and seek within, mentally and spiritually, or to lead the inner life that gives human beings the highest that life on earth can offer.

"How to go into the Silence? First, banish all earthly worries and cares; then relax mind and body, being so comfortable physically that there is no special awareness of the body.

"Then let the mind dwell on all that is fine and noble and holy — lofty ideals, good deeds, the highest thoughts possible and the greatest good the mind can grasp. Do this in a seeking spirit, desiring and asking for guidance, light, insight and wisdom.

"Thus a person advances in ability and character. If it is a daily practice, many helpful truths come that can be practiced for the benefit of self and others.

"Going into the Silence is an antidote to the great restlessness and irritations of modern life that are so destructive that they prevent many from leading happy, healthy and successful lives.

"For everything there is a season, and a time for every purpose under heaven . . . a time to keep silence and a time to speak.

" 'Blessed are they that dwell in thy house: they will still be praising thee." Praising God, they will be still. 'For the Lord God is a sun and shield; the Lord will give grace and glory: no good thing will be withheld from them that walk uprightly.' "

A CALL FROM THE SILENCE

"There are none so lowly but to them can come, in the quiet hour of meditation, the breath of inspiration straight from the Holy Spirit—none so weak but to them can come Divine Strength—none so poor but they may receive a consciousness of the unfailing abundance of right supply.

"Just as the lungs literally breath in human life from the oxygen found in fresh air, so the soul, or spiritual self of man, may breathe in spiritual life from the abundance of Divine Energy which surrounds him at all times.—And just as the lungs must expel the used air in order to make room for the fresh, so must the soul expel all consciousness of lack in order to be receptive to the breath of inspiration waiting to fill it with Life and Joy and Peace Supreme.

"Let go often, then, into that Silent Place of the Soul, that secret Place of the Most High where God in Infinite Love awaits us! There far above all doubts and limitations, one so easily can find God, here he may hear the sublime melody of Life, and may feel the rushing Power of Spirit filling him with God's own Health.

"He who comes to this mountain top of Soul experience will never find his life as drab as it was before. Each task will take on new meaning, and lead to some higher goal. While life will continue to consist of many steps, each will now lead surely upward, nearer and ever nearer to God.

"In the realm of Inspiration man contacts always the highest and best. And that which he contacts is his very own—God's Spiritual Gift to him. His task then is to bring it back into the little world about him and use it for his own better way of living, and for the good of others, that God may be glorified in him.

"Oh, weary ones who walk always upon the low and level and dusty planes of life, look upward! Rise higher in consciousness and find in thine own soul the living breath, the Divine Inflowing Power which awaits you in that higher realm of Spiritual realization.

"Let the Holy Spirit inspire you, lift you up and make you one with Him who is Life Eternal. Breathe of that High and rarified atmosphere which is truly the atmosphere of that Kingdom of Heaven which Jesus declared was so close at hand that it was even within you. Draw into your consciousness the Breath of the Living God.

"Here indeed, is a mystery of the Silence—the mystery of Divine Inspiration." (Fellowship Messenger.)

> "The Lord is in His holy temple: let all the earth keep silence before Him."

> "Be still, and know that I am God."

> "Thou wilt keep him in perfect peace, whose mind is stayed on thee: because he trusteth in thee."

> "But they that wait upon the Lord shall renew their strength; they shall mount up with wings as eagles; they shall run, and not be weary; and they shall walk and not faint."

IN THE STILLNESS OF GOD WITHIN ME I FIND THE STILLNESS THAT COMMANDS MY WORLD.

TWO WORLDS

"The Lord is in His holy temple: let all the earth keep silence before Him." HAB. 2:20

Dr. Rasmus Alsaker says that "The mind builds health by normalizing the functions of the body, by putting all parts of the system into such shape that every organ, every part can work without hindrance. When we are tense, or tightened up, the muscles, glands, and all vital organs cannot work in full; then the circulation stagnates, the glands do not secrete enough, and excessive amounts of toxic matters are made and stored in the body, for the elimination goes bad; for instance, tension constipates.

"Relaxation aids in normalizing the circulation of all the fluids, the secretion, and the excretion of waste; the same is true of a calm, poised, and peaceful mind — it is a wonderful health builder."

We like the command in today's text, "keep silence before Him." It is only as one keeps an inward sense of calm and an awareness of the Presence of God that he can live in perfect mental and physical balance. It is one thing to be able to relax the entire mind and body at stated times — in church, in meditation and in prayer — and quite another thing to carry the respose, tranquility, and power of that relaxation over into a world of confusion and noise.

Viewed from the two aspects of being, man is like a ship on the ocean. He actually lives in two worlds at the same time. On one side are the terrifying storms, threats, fears and fogs of the outer world; on the other side is the mysterious, magnetic world that guides the captain to his goal. We are immersed in the physical body but we cannot live by the physical alone. We must keep an open channel between the body and Spirit. To immunize ourselves against "the slings and arrows of outrageous fortune"—against breakdown, dissolution, trouble and disease—and to heal those ills, we must keep ourselves relaxed in God. Mahatma Ghandi's prescription for living one hundred years was to "Pray three times a day, eat moderately, never become irritated or lose your temper, and be silent one day in seven, as talking uses up nerve energy and gives no chance for meditation."

GOD IS MY STRENGTH AND MY POWER, AND HE MAKETH MY WAY PERFECT BOTH NOW AND EVER MORE.

SPIRITUAL VITAMINS

Read St. John 6:25–35

"The bread of God is he which cometh down from heaven, and giveth life unto the world . . . I am the bread of life: he that cometh to me shall never hunger; and he that believeth on me shall never thirst." JOHN 6:35

There is a belief current among medical men today that the majority of diseases are deficiency diseases, resulting from an insufficient supply of certain chemicals which the body cannot manufacture by itself. Hence, the widespread use of vitamins which are said to make up the deficiency and to keep the body healthy.

Each vitamin has its own specific function. Vitamin A is used to prevent and cure certain weaknesses and diseases of the eyes. Vitamin B is used to raise the resistance of the body and to cure pellagra. Vitamin C is used as preventative and cure for scurvy. Vitamin D is used to promote growth, build bones, and to prevent rickets in children. Vitamin E is used to promote fertility.

But let us think of those other deficiencies which are caused by a lack of spiritual vitamins in the daily diet. Let us think of the people who do not feel well spiritually, those who have allowed doubt, fear, worry, criticism, and bitterness to cloud their vision. Then there is that other group whose members do not grow very much, who are always getting ready to do things but never do them. Spiritual progress and soul growth are unknown to them. They get spiritual anaemia and their consciousness becomes thin, diluted, and sad.

Why is it that we do not experience what Jesus promised us—greater Life, greater Health, greater Prosperity and greater Joy? The fault lies in our daily spiritual diet. We have the prescribed vitamins but we do not use them. We do not practice the Presence of God. We do not keep our eyes single to Truth. We do not exercise our faith and spiritual prerogatives. We do not pray enough, meditate enough, or read the Bible enough. We do not take time to be still and to discipline our thoughts. These are all daily necessities and without them we cannot expect to be whole or well.

Vitamins in religion! Yes, we need them to keep us spiritually successful, healthy, happy, and free.

I GIVE MY WHOLE MIND TO GOD AND MY DEFICIENCIES ARE HEALED.

A NEW BODY

"What? Know ye not that your body is the temple of the Holy Ghost which is in you, which ye have of God, and ye are not your own?" I Cor. 6:19

Our lesson for today teaches that the body is not what we think or believe it to be but is something altogether different. Implanted within the perishable material body which we have mistakenly believed ourselves to be is another body, imperishable and spiritual. St. Paul referred to this Body as "the temple of the Holy Ghost", or body of Christ, and urged us to give it recognition and expression through our minds. The Perfect Body already exists. It exists within every man as the Perfect Expression of the Divine Idea—a New Body behind the old one, Perfection behind imperfection, Reality behind unreality, Permanence behind change, and Continuity behind death. It is perfectly obvious, therefore that there is no excuse for carrying the imperfection of one day into another. If it is true, as science tells us, that the cells of the body are renewed each day, we can prevent their building themselves into the patter of sickness and disease that controlled the cells they are replacing.

How, then, shall we release the old body from its tendency to weakness and disease and raise it to the perfection of its Spiritual Nature? By giving up the old thoughts and beliefs concerning it and by beholding it as it is in Divine Mind. Since the material body is carried in our consciousness as ideas, and since it meticulously reflects every thought, belief, and mental attitude, the way to change the body and bring it into conformity with the Christ standard is to change our idea concerning it. The transformation from the old body to the new begins with a change of consciousness.

Let us go forth this day in the consciousness of a New Body. Let us hold the Perfect Christ body within our physical body until it comes forth as the Perfection which is rightfully ours.

AS I BEHOLD CHRIST WITHIN THE PHYSICAL BODY, MY PERFECT BODY APPEARS.

DIRECTING THE INTELLIGENCE OF THE BODY

"Speak the word only, and my servant shall be healed." MATTHEW 8:8

It is never wise when treating the body to address the body; address the intelligence in the body. Most people think of intelligence as being localized in the brain or central mind, but every organ, cell, and atom of the body has a mind or intelligence of its own. Being under the laws of mind, each quickly carries out any directions given it. When we speak the word, we can expect an immediate response because we are dealing with affinities, or like things.

One of the reasons why there is so much inharmony, tension, and imperfect functioning in the body is that we separate it (through our belief that it is inert matter instead of living substance) from the life of the mankind. We think of mind and body as two separate things and thus break the connection or reciprocal action between them. We restore this harmony and action, when we realize that every part of the body, from the tiniest filament and cell to he largest muscle and system, has a mind and intelligence of its own and that this intelligence responds to and acts upon every thought, belief, feeling, and suggestion of man.

Therefore, when there is pain or discomfort in a certain spot, speak the Truth to the intelligence of that part in firm, strong, God-filled words. Tell it that there is One Perfect Idea behind the ailing organ and that it knows how to keep that organ well, strong, harmonious, and true. Tell it that it not only has the power to keep that organ in perfect rhythm, peace, order, and health, but that you expect it to do so *now*. Then place all the responsibility upon he intelligence in that organ and know that it will be instantly responsive to your word.

A BLESSING FOR THE BODY

Before using this blessing, relax from head to foot (body, mind, and emotions) and direct your attention to the intelligence within the body. I RELAX IN MIND AND BODY AND TRUSTINGLY LET THE DIVINE INTELLIGENCE DO ITS PERFECT WORK IN AND FOR ME. For the time being, stop thinking about your problems, troubles, anxieties, and affairs in the outer world and direct your attention to the intelligence within the organs, nerves, and cells of your body. Quietly affirm: SINCE ALL THE ORGANS, CELLS, AND FUNCTIONS OF MY BODY ARE PERFECT EXPRESSIONS OF INFINITE INTELLIGENCE, I NOW RELAX IN THIS INTELLIGENCE SO THAT I MAY DIRECT THEM AS I WILL.

After a few minutes of this relaxation and realization of every organ and cell as possessing intelligence, speak the truth into this intelligence.

Speak to your eyes as if you expected an instant and intelligent response; tell them that they are made perfect, whole, and strong by the ever-renewing, restoring, vitalizing Life of the Spirit now active in them. "The quickening, vitalizing, lifegiving Christ Life redeems and regenerates you, and you are powerful and perfect." Speak to your ears as you would speak to an intelligent person; tell them that they are quick to hear, to respond, to comprehend, and to understand. "The quick, swift, discerning power of Spirit is now expressed through you (my ears), and I hear perfectly." Speak to your lungs; tell them that they are strong, perfect, and free. Tell them that they do not believe in colds, congestion, or weakness of any kind. "The equalizing, harmonizing, healing power of the Holy Spirit is now established in you, and you are whole and well."

Speak to your heart; tell it that it is "controlled by Divine Love and understanding," that it is strong, accurate, and fearless and that its action is steady and true.

Speak to your stomach as if it were intelligent; praise it for the capable and efficient work it is doing.

Speak to your nerves in the same manner; tell them that they are not subject to noise, friction, confusion, or discord. "You are harmonized, peaceful, and poised in Spirit and in Truth."

Speak to the intelligence in each of the organs of your body, and tell it that it is working in perfect harmony with every other organ. Compliment, praise, and bless, and each will do its best to live up to your expectations.

Declare often that you have the best body, the best stomach, the best heart, the best nerves, the best blood pressure, etc., in the whole world. Pour into the organs of your body words of praise, power, peace, love, poise, joy, and each one will respond with renewed vigor, activity, and health.

STREAMLINING THE BODY

Read I Cor. 3:16–23

"But I keep under my body, and bring it into subjection." I Cor. 9:27

We like the version of this text given by a little girl to her mother when she returned home from Sunday School: "I keep my soul on top." In a sense, she improved the text, because the surest way to keep the body symmetrical and normal is to keep it in tune with God, to keep Truth at the top.

The metaphysical treatment for removing surplus flesh and bringing the body back to its ideal state has two purposes: to discipline the appetite, and to free the mind from adverse beliefs about the body. If we think of the body as material and subject to material laws, it becomes a material thing to us, affected by the laws of food, materiality, and disease. But St. Paul said, "Know ye not that ye are the temple of God, and that the Spirit of God dwelleth in you?" In other words, know that your body is filled with the activity and Presence of Christ, the Presence of Health, Life, Joy, Substance, and that in this Presence, there can be no obesity, impurity, or disease. Know that this Presence is able to spiritualize the body, to dissolve superfluous flesh, and to redeem it from all false appetites. "We are," as Emerson said, "surrounded by spiritual laws which execute themselves." It is our part to let these laws operate through us without mental interference or opposition.

A TREATMENT FOR OVERCOMING OBESITY

"I am the offspring of God, and I am Spirit. My life is spiritual and not material. My body is not material but spiritual.

The All-Powerful Christ Mind in me perfects the glandular functioning in my body and dissolves all of its superfluous flesh. My appetite and the assimiliation of my food are in Divine Order, and my body manifests the symmetry and perfection of the Perfect Body Idea in the Christ Mind."

AS THE TEMPLE OF GOD, MY BODY IS NORMAL, SYMMETRICAL, AND FREE.

THE INNER MAN IS ALWAYS WELL.

". . . many are weak and sickly among you . . . not discerning the Lord's body." I COR. 11:29–30.

When you are dealing with illness of the body, there are two things which you must keep in mind. First, there are two of you — you and yourself, an outer self and an Inner Self, a "me" and an "I". And second, the Inner or Real, the permanent and abiding Self, is always well. The outer self is the fleshly, mortal, human part of you, the son of man. The Inner Self is the central, eternal, indestructible, living, individuality, the I AM or soul, the Son of God.

The outer man, living in the "me", or personal consciousness (circumference of life), subject to the laws of the flesh, is at the mercy of his temptations, weaknesses, sicknesses, deficiencies, imperfections, insufficiencies, circumstances, and conditions. He is the exact likeness of all his mental attitudes, feelings, thoughts, beliefs, and ideas. The Inner man, the Spirit or Christ, is always well and always victorious over the things of the world. He is changeless and eternal.

If it were not for this changeless principle of individuality, man never would know exactly who he is. He would be himself part of the time and somebody else part of the time. But, through individuality, he continues to be himself all the time. "Be ye transformed by the renewing of your mind [change of thought]" does not refer to the Inner Man, but to the outer man. The Inner Man, made in the Image and Likeness of God, being above thought, cannot be affected or changed by thought. The outer man, however, is just the reverse. Being an expression of thought, he can be changed, modified, or transformed by thought.

The discerning of he Lord's body (individuality or soul), therefore, is a mater of living at the Center (in the consciousness of the Divine Image), and radiating from that Center the unceasing, abundant life, vigor, and health of the Real man, who is perpetually whole, well, and strong. How do you live at the Center? By understanding (becoming conscious) that the Inner Man is always well and that you yourself are the Inner Man; by holding this realization until the Inner Man is expressed in the outer man, or personality.

What are the benefits of such a realization? There are many, but chief among hem are the speed with which illness is put to flight and the protection which it provides against disease. When you live in the conviction and realization that the Inner Man is always well and that you are that man, you live in a state of perpetual, personal health. Every thought will then be constructive, restorative, corrective, upbuilding, and elevating, and absolute health and wholeness must result.

THE TEMPLE OF THE HOLY SPIRIT

"What? Know ye not that your body is a temple of the Holy Ghost which is in you?" COR. 6:19

Your body is a temple of the Living God. It is a part of the Universal Intelligence, which is always well. Every cell is alive and vibrant with the Intelligence of God. Therefore, the cells which make up your body have the power to produce perfect health, and to correct any imperfection that may be lurking in your thought.

Never speak of your body or of any of its functions in any but the most complimentary, glowing, and approving terms. Never expect it to be anything but well, strong, vigorous, and ready for any call upon it. Have faith in your body at all times, and make your faith so strong that it becomes the animating center of every cell.

Since your body always lives up to your expectation of it, expect it to be radiant and healthy under all circumstances. Recognize that your expectation of wholeness is your greatest preventive against sickness and disease. Expect your body not only to perform every one of its functions perfectly but to maintain a physical endurance equal to every need. No matter what the present condition of your body is, never think of it as impaired, weak, failing, or inferior in any way; instead, bless it at all times. Praise and blessing build it up; vilification and slander break it down.

Watch your thoughts, feelings, and words when speaking about your body; see to it that they contribute to its well-being, that they increase its life and freedom. This practice will reduce sickness to a minimum and add years to your life. Stop talking about high blood pressure, weak lungs, shattered nerves, sluggish liver, imperfect kidneys, etc.; instead use praise. The result will be that you will sleep better, your body will feel better, look better, act better, and serve you better.

"YE ARE A TEMPLE OF THE HOLY SPIRIT."

REALIZING THE BEST OF YOURSELF

"I, if I be lifted up, will draw all men unto me." JOHN 12:32

1. The first step in realizing the best in yourself is to change your consciousness of yourself. Instead of thinking of yourself as weak, sinful, poor, limited, and helpless, think of yourself as strong, good, prosperous, successful, and free. Know too that what you inwardly believe yourself to be will be built into your life by the creative processes within you.

2. The second step is to know that you are supported by a power that will rush to your aid in any emergency and deliver you—a power that can dissolve and dispel any inharmonious condition in your life.

3. The third step is to face life constructively and to maintain the attitude that attracts the good things of life. You must know and believe that fate is always on your side, always for you, and never against you. Never recognize nor admit bad luck, and never slander yourself in any way.

4. The fourth step is to think always of your divine possibilities, and never of your shortcomings, weaknesses, deficiencies, failures, blunders, or mediocrity. Always appeal to the Inner possible man, and your life will be one continuous round of blessings.

5. The fifth step is to keep your mind off self and on God. Do this not only because it is ego-deflating, but because it keeps you facing toward your goal, towards fulfillment, towards realization, and towards acceptance.

6. The sixth step is to know that no matter what may befall you there is always something greater in you than anything that may be beholding you back. There

is something in you that is bigger than anything that can happen to you — something superior to every belief in inferiority.

7. The seventh step is to give up your egocentric fixations and make yourself significant and important in Christ. Lie above yourself by identifying yourself with those things which take you out of and away from yourself. Be obsessed with the things that unify life. The really important people in the world are those with the smallest egos.

8. The eighth step is always to be "present" in whatever you are thinking, saying, or doing. If you are shaking hands with somebody, be present in your eyes. If you are conversing with somebody, be present in your voice.

9. The ninth step is to accept your Inner Self and live by it. Never seek personal notice, admiration or approval, Never try to be impressive, and never try to attract the attention of others.

10. The tenth step is mentally to renounce ownership over everything. Stop talking about what belongs to you; talk about what you belong to. Find your real self by acknowledging that in your self there is no importance or significance — that you have no life or possessions of your own, for all belong to God.

THE ONLY POWER

"Let every soul be subject unto the higher powers. For there is no power but of God." ROMANS 13:1

Several years ago an experiment was made at one of our great Universities to determine the lifting power of a squash seed.

When the squash had matured sufficiently, it was harnessed to an instrument that registered its power. The harness was increased at various periods of its growth, and when the squash finally broke its rinds, it was lifting a dead weight of five thousand pounds. The physicist tells us that the lifting power of a quart of dried beans is a ton. A rose bush grew through the wall of China. Mushrooms have tilted over great rocks. Hypnotized men have supported hundreds of pounds.

Now, consider what it would mean to use such power consciously. POWER! What a glorious thing it is! Not the personal power men struggle for, but the Power of God! The Power of Life! The Power of Love! The Power of Faith! The Power of Truth! The Power for Good! The Power to Heal! The Power to lift us up unharmed and untouched through every adverse situation! The Power that makes us greater than anything that can happen to us!

You have this Power NOW. It is within you, through you, and around you. You live in it and move through it all the time. It is pressing in upon you, waiting to be used. You are charged with it. It is in you and you are in It, and nothing is impossible to It. You have the Power to attract anything that you need, the Power to heal, the Power to bless, the Power to forgive, the Power to be dauntless and free. You have he Power to think as you will, to do what you want to do, and to be what you want to be. Power assures you of mastery over worry, fear, disorder, discord, and bondage. Rise up, then, in the faith of one who knows that he has All Power, and declare your freedom from every adverse condition in your life

GOD, THE GOOD, OMNIPOTENT IS THE ONLY POWER IN MY LIFE.

SOME THOUGHTS ON DEMONSTRATION

The proper application of Truth will always justify your hope and faith.

There is an objective and subjective element in every problem or disagreeable situation which confronts us. The objective manifestation (unpleasant or threatening situation) is always the outpicturing of negative, chaotic, and undisciplined thoughts and attitudes.

It is never wise to attack the effects of limp or chaotic thinking, therefore, while ignoring the mental antecedents or causes which produced them.

Since difficulties, obstacles, troubles, problems, conditions, and limitations coincide with the material plane of false appearances and effects, the more firmly we keep our consciousness centered in God, the less power our unpleasant, objective experiences will have.

Since God knows no time, there should never be anxiety or hurry in our work. Hurry and anxiety in spiritual practice are evidence of lack of confidence in the infallibility of Truth. The attitude that brings noteworthy results is the calm trust that sees beyond delay and frustration, sees nothing but the instant manifestation and precipitation of God's Word and Substance.

The purpose of treatment is two-fold — to remove the present cause (subjective belief in evil which produces the effect) and to establish a new cause more favorable to our wishes and needs. Remember, however, that the effect will not change until our thought changes.

Demonstrations come thick and fast when true thinking becomes habitual and when the positive in our minds preponderate over the negatives. We shall get our demonstrations then by ignoring the false appearance (putting it entirely out of mind), and by giving our comprehensive faith and attention to the new conditions we are seeking to bring forth. When the subconscious cause is changed and centered in the new ideal and kept centered there, the outer manifestation cannot do other than conform to it.

The next step is to keep the subconscious mind free to concentrate its power with a minimum of interference from the surface mind while the new ideal is becoming real.

The final step is to know that what you are ready for is ready for you.

Since all causes are mental or subjective, you should never be upset when the metaphysician tells you that there is no evil, even when everything in your life is apparently going wrong. "Throw your mental power on the side of Truth and realize that there is no evil in the sight of God. Then you will be working constructively on the cause side and your efforts will produce harmony in the outer world. When we judge by appearances, we are not doing anything to change appearances, but when we know he Truth and affirm it, we are doing a definite work in changing appearances."

THEY SUPPOSED

Read St. Luke 2:41–52.

"But they, supposing him to have been in the company, went a day's journey." LUKE 2:44

They supposed that Jesus was in the company! In other words, they were taking Him for granted. They assumed that He was with them but His Presence had not been verified, and the result was consternation. His parents sought Him, sorrowing.

It would be impossible to estimate the tremendous loss of life, money and property every year caused by carelessness and unverified suppositions. Just a little neglect, carelessness, or forgetfulness! Just a little too much steam in the boiler, and the building is destroyed. Just a little flaw in the rail, and a train is wrecked. Just a cigarette thrown in the wrong place, and countless acres of valuable timber are burned. Just a little carelessness at the switch, and scores of people are killed.

But that is not all. Think of the many customers lost by neglect, the goods ruined by careless packing, the foods spoiled by delay, the people poisoned by mistakes, the business transactions ruined by careless letter-writing, the promotions lost because of indifference and slipshod thinking. Think of the slow advancement of millions because of loose-jointed mental habits.

"They supposed that Jesus was in the company." They supposed that you knew. They supposed that someone had told you. They supposed that someone else had taken care of it.

What is the cure for these vague suppositions, inaccurate performances, limp thinking, and wandering minds? Just two things: fixity of vision and invincibility of purpose. To make the very minimum of mistakes, we must take nothing for granted. We must be certain and accurate in everything that we do.

I MAKE NO MISTAKES BECAUSE ALL MY AFFAIRS ARE HANDLED THROUGH CHRIST.

A PROPHECY

"Beloved, now are we the sons of God, and it doth not yet appear what we shall be: But we know that, when He shall appear, we shall be like Him; for we shall see Him as He is." I JOHN 3:1

"Two friends in Athens were once discussing the ennobling influence of Greek art. In the course of the conversation one said: 'I came here on a hiking tour with a chap who was not making as much of himself as he should have done. But he went away a changed man, mentally and morally strong; physically perfect. You would never guess what it was that did it.

"H saw a statue of one of the Greek gods in the museum. Studying it closely, he found that it showed certain muscles that he could not find in his own body.

"He told me that he was going to train down till those muscles did show. He stopped drinking and loafing to do it. He took to exercising, walking, rowing, swimming, and boxing.

"By the time the muscles showed out clear and strong, he was so keen over life that he wanted to make the most out of it. And, as I have said, he has done it.

"The vision of physical perfection changed that man's life. He saw what he was, and what he wanted to be. And he went to work and made himself as the statue of that Greek god, with all the hidden strength that is expressed.' "

God's temple is both visible and invisible. "It serves as His abiding place and provides a vehicle for your soul's expression." Within the weak, timid, hesitating, and fearful man, is the strong, courageous, victorious, and triumphant

Son of God—the larger, Possible man you are capable of becoming. There are latent power, undiscovered possibilities, unused resources, locked-up abilities still waiting to come forth.

This is the man you ought to be. This is the man you can be. This is the man you will be. This is your true life. Go forth then and claim this Grander Self as your own.

> BEHOLDING AS IN A MIRROR THE IMAGE OF CHRIST, I AM TRANSFORMED INTO THE SAME IMAGE.

NON-CONFORMITY

Read Rom. 12.

"Be not conformed to this world: but be ye transformed by the renewing of your mind, that ye may prove what is that good, and acceptable, and perfect will of God." ROMANS 12:2

To keep his small son occupied, a father cut a map of the world into small pieces and asked him to put it together again. To the father's amazement, the lad returned promptly with the map put together.

"How did you do it so quickly?" asked the father.

"There was a picture of a man on the other side," replied the boy. "I put the man together, and the world just came together."

The only way to change the world is to change men's thought about it. Thought is both the power and form of all things. The world is but the outer manifestation of inner mental concepts. The circumstances that we attract will always correspond to our mental images. It is important, therefore, that we keep our minds active toward good and inactive toward evil. That is what St. Paul meant by non-conformity to the world.

If our thinking and living do no conform to the Truth, they will be thrown into confusion in the same way that a trial balance is upset by a single mistake. We can neutralize confusion only as we cease to follow error and conform to the Truth.

Our real problem is not the things that seem to be wrong in the outer world: poor health, small income, unpleasant surroundings, and irritating circumstances. The problem is to harmonize our minds with God's Mind, to bring our wills into conformity with His Will, and to bring all our desires, thoughts, words, and acts into harmony with the principles of Truth. In other words to bring man, body, soul, and spirit, into perfect harmony with God.

We should start at once to blot out all the false beliefs and limiting ideas that have cluttered up our lives. Instead of reacting to trouble negatively, we must learn to react positively. We must control our world by controlling our attitudes toward it. If problems are the result of lack of harmony with God, they will be solved only when harmony has been restored.

THE MIND OF GOD NOW ACTIVE IN ME TRANSFORMS MY WORLD INTO A PLACE OF PEACE AND HARMONY.

CAUTION—GOD AT WORK

"My Father worketh hitherto, and I work." JOHN 5:17

A sign frequently seen on streets and highways under construction is "MEN AT WORK." How arresting it would be to come upon a sign on an office door or on a man's desk which read, "CAUTION—GOD AT WORK!" We have never seen such a sign, of course, but it is said that John R. Mott, world famous YMCA leader, who was so busy during World War I that he had to give interviews on sub-ways and surface cars, never failed to spend an hour or more each day with God in prayer. There was no "DO NOT DISTURB" sign hung outside his office door during these conferences with God, but there was always a handkerchief on the floor which no one dared cross.

Where, then, could we hand such a sign to the greatest advantage: "CAUTION—GOD AT WORK?" Why, in our consciousness, of course. One of the difficult things for the average Truth student to realize is that God continues working even after we have stopped, and that He works quite independently of our own efforts. When we plant seeds in the earth, we protect them by putting a fence around them. When we plant spiritual seed-thoughts in the mind, we erect a mental fence to protect them against doubt, worry, and other intruding thoughts from the outside world. We isolate them until the subconscious mind accepts them, and they begin to germinate and grow. The fences are caution signs to remind us that GOD IS AT WORK.

"Ever since my son has been in the army," said a mother, "I have written to him every day. He promised to do the same. Though his daily letter may not arrive, I trust that he has written. Of course, there are dreary days when no mail comes, and other days when accumulated letters arrive; but each knows the other is writing and that is enough for both of us." It is that certainty, you see, which keeps God working in our behalf. It is what St. Paul meant when he said, "Pray without ceasing."

The important thing is not the affirmative answer nor what may be happening on the surface, but our connection with God, our knowledge that He is at work and that the answer will come.

"I HAVE PLANTED, APOLLOS WATERED, AND GOD GAVE THE INCREASE."

"GLORIFY THOU ME"

"And now, O Father, glorify Thou Me with Thine own Self with the glory which I had with Thee before the world was." JOHN 17:5

The solution of undesirable conditions is not found by changing things but by changing ourselves. It is not a question of manipulating outer circumstances, nor of maintaining the *status quo.* The solution is found in recovering something that has been loss—our consciousness of the Presence of God. Conditions, contrary to human belief, are never in our environment but in our minds. They are an overt expression of our attitude toward life.

Jesus never asked God to change anything, remove anything, or destroy anything; he asked only that He manifest the glory of the Father in Himself. He recognized that since conditions were only degrees of forgetfulness of God, they could be changed only by a complete remembering, or by re-centering ourselves in God. We should accept the fact, then, that no matter who we may be, where we are, or what we are doing, conditions will always be just what they are. Since environment is but an extension of ourselves, it can never be other than like itself.

The glory which Jesus sought from God was not power over the world but power over Himself. He was not asking for something that He did not already have, but for something that should be recovered. He did not ask that something be changed, but only that something be restored.

Father, glorify Thou me with the dominion which I had with Thee before this human mind was, before I accepted the idea of separation, before I believed in two powers, before I entered into this mortal flesh of sin, sickness, and trouble, before I allowed myself to be tempted. Help me to see the things and to hear the things which have been here all the time. Help me to be perfect as Thou art Perfect. As I have borne the image of the earthly with all its trouble and suffering, so help me to bear the image of the Heavenly.

"FATHER, GLORIFY THOU ME WITH THINE OWN SELF WITH THE GLORY WHICH I HAD WITH THEE BEFORE THE WORLD WAS."

INVISIBLE SERVANTS

"Behold, I will send my messenger, and he shall prepare the way before me." MAL. 3:1

Our text reminds us of a mighty snow plow clearing a path before us. On both sides of the road, great piles of snow are thrown up so that we may pass. Without the plow, there might have been serious delay: urgent business made to wait, appointments cancelled, personal contacts postponed.

Now, what is this messenger that shall prepare the way before us? Is it some mechanical device like a snow plow or bull-dozer, a walkie-talkie, telephone, telegraph, or radio? No, it is none of these, and yet it is swifter than any of them. It is our spoken word, traveling on an invisible circuit that is faster than light. A radio message is carried around the world in one seventh of a second. But the Word of God is instant.

We have thought of this text solely as prophesying the coming of John the Baptist to open the way before Jesus. Now we know that it connotes a scientific fact concerning our thoughts and words. We are actually sending out these messengers all the time, and they do prepare the way before us. They either make life easy or they make it hard, according to the kind of messengers we send forth. If we speak negative words, they create obstacles where none exist. If we speak positive words, they make the crooked places straight. Always our word has he exact meaning and amount of power that we put into it; it always initiates activities like the thought that we send out.

How careful we should be, then, in selecting the kind of words we send out! If we do not like the way that has been prepared for us, we can change it by choosing different messengers to do our work. Let us send only messengers of faith, love, hope, and self-confidence.

DIVINE LOVE GOES BEFORE ME AND PREPARES THE WAY.

THE LIMITING FACTOR

". . . other (seed) fell into good ground, and brought forth fruit, some an hundredfold, some sixtyfold, some thirtyfold." MATTHEW 13:8

When the farmer speaks of the "limiting factor" in the fertility of the soil, he means that things are not in balance. The land may have some of every needed requirement for a good crop, sun, food, water, depth, proper chemistry, tillage, freedom from pests, and the yield still be very poor.

Elements must properly balance. There cannot be too much of one thing, and too little of another. Conditions may appear right on the surface, but if there is disproportion at one point, there will be disproportion in the whole. It is obvious, therefore, that "what good land needs for its proper fertility is an adjusted proportion of its own best qualities."

Here is a parable from the soil of a law of spiritual demonstration. The "limiting factor" explains why some succeed in metaphysical science and others fail. When we fulfill the requirements of prayer but fail to get results, it is probable that things are out of balance. We are overdoing some things and underdoing others. There may be too much hope and not enough practical action, or too much wishing and not enough faith. Perhaps there is a discrepancy between the prayer and performance, between the demand and acceptance. We may ask for something with our lips and deny it in our hearts. We are not in focus. All our forces are not moving toward our goal. We provide the mental equivalent through which the Divine Energy is to flow, but we do not eliminate the static and friction of negative thoughts. We try to change conditions without changing our consciousness. We use too many words and do not put enough meaning into them.

Always discover the limiting factor and then remove it as soon as possible. When our thinking is fifty-one percent positive, we shall begin to get results.

I CANNOT BE SEPARATED FROM MY GOOD BECAUSE I AM UNIFIED WITH GOD.

THE THREE MONKEYS

"And why beholdest thou the mote that is in thy brother's eye, but considerest not the beam that is in thine own eye?" MATT. 7:3

"One of the greatest metaphysical lessons ever taught is that of the three monkeys: See no evil, Hear no evil, Speak no evil. They remind us that we see things not as they are, hear things not as they are, and judge things not as they are, but as we are. These truths are self-evident; when we understand them, we shall be very careful of our judgments and criticisms of others. Why? Because in making them, we are simply making X-ray plates that reflect our own capacities, qualities, and states of mind. If we do not want to expose these hidden negatives to others, we shall either keep still or temper what we say.

Perhaps you have never compared your eyes and ears and lips to the reporters on a newspaper who report what they see and hear. The editor, however, determines what is printed. So it is with us. Our eyes and ears bring vibrations to us, and the personal mind (judging sense) interprets these vibrations and makes deductions in accord with our inner mental standards. Good and evil are not inherent in circumstances, happenstances, or conditions, but in the mind that judges or interprets them. When the mind imputes evil, it stamps upon another a quality that emanates from itself.

Shakespeare said, "There is nothing good or bad but thinking makes it so." We should remember this and practice searching for the good, practice being kind and generous in our judgments of others and sparing in our criticism of what they say and do.

"For with what judgment ye judge, ye shall be judged: and with what measure ye mete, it shall be measured to you again." Everyone has to make a choice between the law of attraction and the law of repulsion. Condemnation and criticism repel; approbation and praise attract.

> THROUGH THE SPIRIT OF TRUTH WITHIN ME,
> I KNOW, SEE, HEAR, AND SPEAK ONLY TRUTH.

THE SECOND COMING OF CHRIST

"I will come again, and receive you unto myself; that where I am, there ye may be also." JOHN 14:3

There are two negative erroneous beliefs which every Truth student must drop from his mind before he can embody the Presence of Christ. One is the mistaken idea that salvation centers in the personality of Jesus instead of in the Christ Spirit which He possessed. The other is the belief that the Christ Principle (the only begotten son) disappeared with the fleshly part of Jesus and will some day return. Both of these ideas, so widely held by orthodox Christians today, not only do great violence to the basic teachings of Jesus and to the character and nature of God, but they explain why Christianity is so impotent, colorless, and lacking in resources. For centuries, we have been taught to follow Jesus instead of embodying the Christ.

Now, ask yourself how the Omnipresent, the Omnipotent, the Omniscient can be relegated to some distant place and some future time and how the finite, physical body can occupy and pervade a universe that is Infinite, that is essentially spiritual?

Jesus said that He (the Christ) would return, and His promise has already been fulfilled. It was fulfilled at Pentecost but not, as visionaries and waiting congregations expected and hoped, in trailing clouds of glory, pageantry, pomp and public display. Did they recognize His first Advent? No! Did they recognize the Second Advent? No! And why not? Because they did not know what glory is. There was glory, unspeakable glory, in the manger at Bethlehem, but most people passed it by. They missed it because they were unaccustomed to it. They were, as most of us are now, looking for something else.

Now, listen to Jesus again and you will understand why the tense of His words makes all the difference in the results of our practices. "Lo, I am with you always." Does that sound as if the Christ has been away from us for 2000 years? Certainly not. The Christ is here. The Kingdom of Heaven is at hand. Now is the day of Salvation. The first Advent was Immanuel — God with us. The Second Advent is God within us. When we have the Christ in the possessive cause, the second coming has taken place.

"IT IS NO LONGER I THAT LIVE, BUT CHRIST LIVETH IN ME."

THE NORTH AND SOUTH POLES

"For to be carnally minded is death; but to be spiritually minded is life and peace." ROM. 8:6

To make today's lesson clear, let us think of man's mind as a horseshoe magnet like those we played with as children. It has two sides, or poles. One is known as the north, or positive pole; the other is the south, or negative pole. "A mysterious current or magnetic flux or energy which is resident in the magnet flows out from the north or positive pole to an iron bar, a nail, or any other suitable metal object being used in the experiment. It passes through this object and returns to the south or negative pole of the magnet. The result is that the metal object is drawn or attracted to the magnet.

"The nail or bar of iron does not go to the magnet simply because the magnet wants it to come or needs it. IT GOES BECAUSE OF WHAT THE MAGNET SENDS OUT. It goes because of the invisible energy which the magnet radiates.

"Moreover, the nail or bar has no choice in the matter. Under the working of the law of attraction, it is COMPELLED to move toward the magnet. And, remember, that this is strictly in accordance with the working of a natural law, a LAW OF GOD, even though few understand it or have put it to work.

"And the mystery of it is that the MAGNET, of itself, does nothing. The real work is done by the silent, unseen energy which flows out from its north or positive pole, and which is directed toward that which the magnet desires."

If you will now think of your consciousness as the magnet of your life, you will see why it is that the Universe does not give you what you ask, expect, want or think you ought to have, but why it gives you only what you are. Since Life is a state of consciousness, since it is governed by an impersonal law, it will always attract conditions like itself and repel conditions which are unlike itself. The real secret of getting what is wanted on any plane, therefore, is to mentally embody what we want within our consciousness.

THE SPIRIT OF GOD NOW ACTIVE IN MY MIND ATTRACTS ONLY GOOD INTO MY WORLD. BEING FILLED WITH THIS SPIRIT OF GOD'S RICH ABUNDANCE, I AM AN IRRESISTIBLE MAGNET THAT DRAWS TO ME ALL MATERIAL THINGS NEEDFUL TO MY COMPLETENESS AND PERFECTION.

THE SIGN OF THE WINE

"Every man at the beginning doth set forth good wine; and when men have well drunk, then that which is worse; but thou hast kept the good wine until now. This beginning of miracles did Jesus in Cana of Galilee." JOHN 2:10, 11

The changing of the water into wine is not only one of the most human and colorful of the New Testament miracles, but one of the most interesting. The word the evangelist uses for "miracles" is *signs.* This suggests that we must look for some metaphysical or spiritual significance in the story.

The place of the miracle is in Cana of Galilee. The occasion is a wedding feast in an obscure home. We are not told who the bride and groom were, but we know that it was a wedding feast and that Jesus was there. It was customary in those days for the bridegroom to furnish his guests with wine. Quite naturally, the bridegroom was embarrassed when the supply of wine ran out; it was to save him from this embarrassment that Jesus stepped into the breach.

How did Jesus perform this miracle? Through the cooperation of the servants. It was they who poured water into the pots, and they who drew wine out of them. What should this signify to us? Christ's method of meeting our needs and transforming our lives waits upon our obedience and upon our cooperation with Him. When He would feed five thousand people, He must have the cooperation of the disciples and a little boy who was carrying his lunch. When He heals a paralytic, He must have the cooperation of his loyal friends.

God put us here to be channels for His Good. God's work is done. He is both the Law and the Supply. Our part is to cooperative with the law, to receive and distribute the supply.

One of the things beginning Truth students fail to see is that they must take the first step. Man thinks, prays, or speaks; and then God acts. The Law works for man when man begins to obey and cooperate with the law. How is this obedience and cooperation carried out? By keeping our faith centered in God and by refusing to give attention or importance to anything unlike Him. "Thou shalt love the Lord thy God with all thy heart, and with all thy soul, and with all thy mind," and "Thou shalt love thy neighbor as thyself."

A miracle is simply the occurrence of an event which takes place outside the time process. It happens *now* instead of at some future time.

THE POWER OF BLESSING

"Love your enemies, do good to them that hate you, bless them that curse you, and pray for them which despitefully use you and persecute you." LUKE 6:27, 28

One of the most difficult things for persecuted and injured persons to do is bless those who have caused them trouble, to pray for those who have hurt them, to forgive those who have been unkind, and to love those who have been hateful. It is so much easier to resent and retaliate. We think it is a mark of manhood or womanhood to do so. Our reputation is at stake and must be defended. Our character is being attacked and must be vindicated. Our feelings have been hurt and must be assuaged. We demand justice—an eye for an eye and a tooth for a tooth. We draw the sword of our tongue or the arrows of our thoughts and send these poison missiles in every direction.

It was just such situations as these which Jesus had in mind when He spoke the words of our text. "Vengeance is mine, I will repay saith the Lord." "Overcome evil with good." These are statements of the law of cause and effect. It is not God or man who punishes the evil doer, but the law of cause and effect. Then why should we get all upset over what people say or do? Why should we try to "get even" and, by our negative reactions, give others power to rob us of our freedom, happiness, and peace of mind? If the law always takes care of every injustice and returns to man what is due him, why shouldn't we by blessing and by prayer cooperate with the Power moving within the situation?

Jesus knew the power of blessing, and that is why He gave it such a prominent place in the Sermon on the Mount. It is the most effective means not only of stripping an enemy of his power over us, but of changing our attitude towards him. Why not build a new world by utilizing this power constantly in our prayer, thought, and speech?

Bless everything and everybody at all times and under all circumstances. Bless the people whom you meet. Bless the adverse circumstances and the unpleasant conditions in your life. Bless your body many times a day. Bless every function and organ. Bless your home, your food, your clothes, your bed, your automobile.

Bless the things that go wrong and the things that are right. Keep up the practice of blessing, and you will be surprised how people and conditions will change and how new blessings will come into your life.

HOW TO DEAL WITH ENEMIES

"For perhaps he [Onesimus] *departed for a season, that thou shouldest receive him for ever; not now as a servant, but above a servant, a brother beloved, specially to me, but how much more unto thee, both in the flesh and in the Lord."* PHILEMON 15, 16

"Cooks say that if the ingredients of a certain sauce get too hot, a little cream added will keep it from curdling and bring it back." When friends become enemies and the relations between them get too hot, a third element is need to bring them back to normal. The enemy, yourself, and God: that is the divine pattern for overpowering adversaries and for eliminating enemies. "When human relations are like lines between two points, they are flat. When they are like the sides of a triangle with God at the apex, they stand up."

In yesterday's text from the Sermon on the Mount, Jesus outlined four ways in which to overcome one's enemies and to bring the God factor into sterile relations. Love them. Bless them. Do good to them. Pray for them. To many, these statements will sound puerile, but let us see.

1. "LOVE YOUR ENEMIES." This does not mean to put your arms round your enemies or to send them

Robert A. Russell

candy or flowers, but to unify yourself with God. It means to erase all discord, hate, animosity, conflict, and confusion in your mind and to dissolve all critical, bitter, revengeful, irritable, fretful, and antagonistic thoughts within the consciousness. "Love your enemies" means to change your attitude and establish peace and harmony within your mind.

2. "BLESS THEM THAT CURSE YOU." Curses are turned into blessings through our steadfast knowledge that God is all, and that enmity has no power to hurt us or to hurt him who sends it. If we remain uncritical in our attitude and replace hate with love, we shall turn our curses into blessings.

3. "DO GOOD TO THEM THAT HATE YOU." This command is fulfilled WITHIN; we do good to our enemies by perceiving them as perfect expressions of divine Life, or Peace, Love, and Harmony.

4. "PRAY FOR THEM WHICH DESPITE FULLY USE AND PERSECUTE YOU." Praying for an enemy not only changes our attitude and feeling towards him, but "lifts him to a higher plane of consciousness and sets him free; it is God's Law of Love in action. We speak the word of peace, forgiveness, Diving fulfillment, and harmony."

"BECAUSE THERE ABIDES IN MY HEART A STEADFAST LOVE FOR THE LORD MY GOD, AND BECAUSE I TRUST IN HIM AND HIS PROMISES OF SURE DELIVERANCE, I SHALL REMAIN IN QUIETNESS AND IN CONFIDENCE, UNTROUBLED AND UNMOVED, THOUGH ENEMIES RISE AGAINST ME, AND FALSE FRIENDS BETRAY ME."

HOW CAN I KNOW GOD?

"In Him we live, and move, and have our being." ACTS 17:28

Beginning Truth students often ask, "How can I know God?" The answer is, "by practicing His Presence." "And how do I practice His Presence?" "By letting the Spirit of Christ within you express Himself through you."

The chief end of man is not alone to glorify God in the conscious mind, but also to express His attributes of Life, Love, Truth, and Power. These attributes are already within us, but they must be released, materialized, and expressed before they can become visible. Our answer to this question should be amplified by saying that the way to know God is through association, identification, imitation, appropriation, and expression.

If I want God to think through my brain, see through my eyes, hear through my ears, speak through my mouth, and feel through my body, I must first let Him think through my intelligence. If I want to attract the best from others and from my environment, I must be conscious that these same attributes are being expressed back to the world from me.

In other words, I must express God's All-Presence. I must see, feel, and express Him in everything I think, say, or do. I must find Him first in the persons and things close to me; then I shall see Him in ever widening circles. It is just like throwing a stone into a placid lake of water. The ripples will spread in ever widening circles until they reach the farther-most shore.

"God is Spirit" and to express the right spirit in every thing you think, say, and do is to demonstrate Good only. "God is Life," Have faith in It. Believe that It is powerful enough to penetrate and to dispel every inharmonious condition. Life multiplies through expression. It diffuses Its light, Its vitality, Its strengthening, adjusting power to every part of your world. "God is Truth." When you conform to It in every thought, word, and act, you will know that the Truth demonstrates Itself in you.

"God is Love." This is as high as you can go. Love is the greatest attribute of God—the Principle of all healing, wholeness, and completeness, and the fulfillment of every human need. "God is Power." Join yourself to It, and let It operate through you wisely.

IN THE QUIETNESS OF SOLITUDE I REALIZE MY COMPLETE ONENESS WITH GOD.

ASH WEDNESDAY

"The voice of one crying in the wilderness, Prepare ye the way of the Lord, make his paths straight. Every valley shall be filled, and every mountain and hill shall be brought low; and the crooked shall be made straight, and the rough ways shall be made smooth; and all flesh shall see the salvation of God." ISAIAH 40:3, 4, 5

Ash Wednesday is the open door to Lent. It is so called from the ancient custom of imposing ashes on the forehead of the faithful as a symbol of repentance and self-denial and in recognition of the transitoriness of human life. These were not ashes in the ordinary sense of the word, but ashes made from the burning of palms from the previous Palm Sunday.

Lent, like every other season in the church year, has two sides—a giving-up side and an acquiring side. The theological mind thinks of it chiefly in terms of subtractions and deletions believing that it grows by what it gives up. The metaphysical mind, on the other hand, knows that this is only half the process. The other half is substitution and appropriation, for Truth must be supplied in place of the error which has been dropped. Lent is a season of both subtractions and additions. It is a time, not only of changing the mind out of the old but of changing it into the new, of adding something that will make our lives truer, stronger, more triumphant and more effective, of appropriating the riches of Spirit. It should not be a season of depression, despondency, and sorrow, but of happiness, jubilance, and joy.

The real purpose of Lent is stated in St. Paul's words: "Let this mind be in you, which was also in Christ Jesus." In other words let God think through your mind, feel through your senses, speak through your lips, hear through your ears, see through your eyes, judge through your Christ, act through your body, pray through your soul, and decide through your consciousness.

Lent calls for a change of identification and allegiance. No longer acting with personality through the human mind, you now act with Christ through Divine Mind. It is a change of self — a shift in the center of gravity. You simply align yourself day by day with your God-Nature and make that dominant in your life. You let Christ reach far back in your consciousness to wake the Real Man and all those finer qualities in your being which have so long been hidden.

THE ETERNAL SPIRIT OF GOD BIDS ME ARISE
AND WALK IN NEWNESS OF LIFE.

PRAYER CHANGES THINGS

"Prayer changes things." These words in electric lights high above one of our modern down town tabernacles seem to imply that the fundamental purpose of prayer is to change things. To the casual observer it gives the impression that prayer is some clever and magic device for drawing personal benefits from reluctant and unwilling hands, a sort of magician's hat out of which to draw rabbits, money, flowers, and colored silk handkerchiefs.

Please do not misunderstand me. I am not saying that petition has no place in prayer, but that those who put it first are very likely to be disappointed in the results. Jesus has given petition a very central place in the Lord's Prayer, but not the first place. The first place must be given to the Kingdom of God or to fellowship with Him. Henry Ward Beecher wrote: "Is it not apt to vulgarize and cheapen prayer to think of it only in terms of getting things material? Would you permit a man to call himself your friend who had no higher conception of friendship than to ask for favors?" There is deep meaning in this question, for there is no surer way to ruin friendship than always to be asking for something. It is, as Joseph R. Sizoo says, "like writing a letter home only when you want to borrow money."

Prayer does not so much "change things," correct mistakes, cure ills, overcome difficulties or solve problems, as it removes causes. Much has been written on the subject of prayer in recent years—what is is, how it works, and what it does, but what we most need now is a book on what prayer is not. How should such a book begin? It would surely start out by saying that prayer is not for the purpose of asking God to change His Mind toward us but to help us know that His Mind is in us, and to make us sensitive to His will. It is not asking for benefits, blessings, and favors which we do not deserve or which He is not willing to give, because He is more willing to give than we are to ask. It is not a draft on the Bank of Heaven but an attitude toward life. It is formula but an experience. It is not a set of spiritual setting-up exercises or autosuggestion. It is not telling God what He already knows or bribing Him to change His attitude toward us.

Prayer is a commital of our minds and will to Him, the putting of ourselves in the way of being found by Him. Changing things is only secondary. The first thing is to change ourselves in order that God can have the right of through us.

SHIFT FROM NEUTRAL INTO GEAR

Dr. Harry Emerson Fosdick has told the story about a church sexton up in Maine who, somewhat like the old woman of shoe and children fame, had so many bosses that he didn't know what to do. All of the members of that little church who made any financial contribution whatsoever took it upon themselves. to be individual bosses for the poor sexton.

"One day when someone asked the sexton how he was able to stand all this multiplicity of bossing, he replied, 'Oh, I just shift my mind into neutral and then let them push me around wherever they want to."

There is humor in this story, but there is also pathos and tragedy, too. One of the chief reasons why there is so much human misery, trouble, sorrow in the world today is that, like this sexton, most of us are living, thinking, speaking, and acting in neutral. Having no direction or control of our own, we are directed and controlled by others. We are allowing ourselves to be pushed around by personalities, conditions, circumstances, fears, jealousies, nervousness, unhappiness, mediocrity and dissipation of energy.

Then, how shall we shift from neutral into gear so that we are no longer dominated by "the slings and arrows of outrageous fortune?" By a continuous and faithful practice of the Presence of God, and by the habitual acknowledgment and affirmation that He is the only power in our lives. We become, not circumstance-directed, but God-directed. We are no longer subject to a power over us but to a Power within us. We shall no longer believe ourselves to be creatures of the dust, but we shall know ourselves for what we are. We shall no longer look upon our body as an instrument for drudgery, a puppet for others to push around, but shall see it as an open channel for God's great Power. We shall no longer think of the mind as a medium for "individual bosses" to think through, but shall recognize it as a great capacity for Knowledge, Guidance, and Love from the Fountain-Head of all Wisdom Itself.

SUCCESSFUL CHRISTIAN MARRIAGE

"For this cause shall a man leave father and mother, and shall cleave to his wife; and they twain shall be one flesh." MATTHEW 19:5

"Religion is the only unifying and ever-present force which can help to solve the inevitable moral and intellectual conflicts of parents, children, and society at large. In a world of change and rebellion to authority, God is the only fixed point." (Henry C. Link)

The great reason why so many marriages go on the rocks today is not because of physical incompatibility, but because of psychic incompatibility. There is nothing to perpetuate the companionship, to integrate it, and hold it together. There is no religion, no centrality, and no "disciplined corporate living." Centered only in two imperfect individuals with no cohesive power between them, marriage soon goes to pieces.

We stand aghast at the alarming number of divorces in America today, the broken homes, and blighted lives; but the fact remains that unless the Spiritual enters into the marriage contract, it cannot be enduring or successful.

We are giving a few simple rules in today's lesson, not only for the purpose of strengthening marriage ties still intact, but also to aid in salvaging and reuniting those which have been broken.

First: At least once a month read the service by which you were united in marriage; ponder particularly the promises which you and your mate made to God and to each other. That service ties up in an agreement not two lives but three: yourself, your partner, and God. God is not only the Center and foundation of Christian marriage, but the unifying Force which harmonizes and makes the man and woman one. To live without God is to lose not only the sacramental quality of marriage but its spiritual nature.

Second: Keep God at the center of your marriage and at the head of your household by giving Him first place in your lives. Start your day and end it with scripture reading, prayer, and unifying affirmations of Truth. Avoid friction and clash of human wills by keeping His Will supreme.

Third: Do not try to reform your partner nor to make him what you think he ought to be. Do not nag, criticize, compare, or find fault. Be attentive, be generous with appreciation and praise, and be fully informed on the sexual side of marriage.

FAMILY RELATIONSHIPS WITHIN THE HOME

"One thing is needful: and Mary hath chosen that good part." Luke 1 0:42

In reading my *Forward Day by Day* I ran on to this story: Someone asked a parson which he'd rather have for a wife, Mary or Martha. He said, "Martha before dinner. Mary afterwards."

"It seems to me that Mary's 'good part' was simply in her learning something from Christ, while letting her sister work off her nervous pre-occupation with the dinner. The center of Martha's concern was the house; the center of Mary's concern was Christ. Mary was not lazy; she was centered in Him. Martha was not industrious; she was centered in the dinner. Mary believed that Christ came before everything.

"That really is the secret of a happy home, and of creative human relations within it. If everybody is captain, and nobody is crew, as is the case in many homes, where is the last word to be found? If Christ is Captain, and we all look to Him for orders, each one listening, each one obeying, every job will get done, and in the right spirit. Nobody likes 'bossy' people in the home, or nagging people, or uncooperative ones. No matter how good a job Mom or Dad make of running the home, we would all be better off if we listened to God for our orders.

"Family prayers will be a lot more real if we all learn to keep quiet for awhile, asking God what He wants us to do; if we share with each other the things we feel most deeply; and if we are each obedient to what God tells us."

Someone has said that the two most difficult places in the world in which to be a Christian are the home and the church.

The reason for this is at once clear-too much self, too much human will, not enough God and not enough love.

When Fielding H. Yost, grand old man of football, was asked what qualities make a great football team he said, "The greatest of these is Love." "Love of pals," he said, "love of the game, love of the school the boys play for." Hate is a negative force, while love is positive and makes for strength, for the best fighting type of man, especially when it comes to fighting for the things in which one is interested. With it go truth, courage, and faith, all positive forces.

If love, then, is the greatest quality in building a great football team, it is an even greater quality in building a great home team. When the individual members of the family put God at the head, and each other first, and establish their thinking under the law of Divine Love, the relationships of the home will be in perfect order, peaceful and harmonious at all times and under all circumstances.

> EVERY THOUGHT OF MY MIND AND EVERYTHING IN MY HOME IS UNDER GOD'S LOVING DIRECTION.

SUGGESTIONS FOR HUSBANDS

"He that is faithful in that which is least, is faithful also in much: and he that is unjust in the least, is unjust also in much." LUKE 16:10

Since many marital rifts, ruptures, and separations have their origin in some failure of the husband—some neglect, indifference, preoccupation or lack of attention to small necessities, we are listing some of these failures and their antidotes in today's lesson, in the hope that those who need them will not only find them but profit by them to the end that marriage now stagnant and impotent may quickly be reclaimed and restored to their original lustre and beauty:

1. Keep your courtship and romanticism alive. You can do this in two ways: by being thoughtful, attentive, tender, and kind, and by remembering your wife with special gifts and sentiments on special days, anniversaries, birthdays, etc.
2. Never express irritability or make complaint at the breakfast table, and never indulge harsh words or criticize your wife before the children or others. REFUSE TO ARGUE.
3. Provide your wife with "an independent happiness fund." It is not enough to provide money for household expenses. Your wife must have money for herself, to spend as she sees fit.
4. Be considerate, patient, and kind, especially when your wife is nervous and tired. Try to understand her changing moods and to help her through them.
5. Spend as many evenings as possible at home, and include your wife in a generous portion of your play hours.
6. Take an active interest in your wife's social religious, intellectual, and other activities, and in her views on your own and other problems.
7. Never be indifferent to your wife, especially in public.
8. Take nothing for granted. Be generous with praise and admiration, and thank her for all the little services she performs for you.
9. Go to church with your wife. Support the church, and enter into its activities with her.

SUGGESTIONS FOR WIVES

"Likewise, ye, wives, be in subjugation to your husbands; that, if any obey not thee word, they also may without the word be won by the conversation n of the Wives." I PETER 3:1

Successful wifehood consists not alone in finding the right husband, being an attractive and charming wife, having a beautiful home, children and money, but in being the right kind of woman. Successful marriage is not a happenstance but an achievement. When the glamour of courtship and the ecstacy of romance have worn off, there are always adjustments to be made, imperfections to be healed, deficiencies to be supplied, and faults to be corrected. Then, who shall make these daily adjustments and take effective counter measures to meet them? Why, the wife, of course. She will do it "in the spirit of understanding, tolerance, and love." Here are some suggestions:

1. Give your husband freedom of thought at all times and under all circumstances; give him a certain privacy in his own life. A void curiosity about his mail; never pry into his activities, or try to think or make decisions for him, and never try to select his friends.
2. Always present a solid mother-and-father front to the children and never side with a child against its father.
3. Familiarize yourself with your husband's business and other interests so that you can discuss them intelligently and helpfully with him.
4. Never compare the achievements of your husband unfavorably with those of other men. Never criticize him for his mistakes; if failure and disappointment come, help him to meet them bravely.

5. Always treat your husband's relatives with the same consideration that you give your own, and never adopt a martyr complex or a holier-than-thou state of mind. If wrong, admit it, and express sorrow.

6. Make your consciousness of God's Presence so strong through daily prayer and meditation that you can meet whatever comes up in quietness, confidence, love, and understanding.

7. Do not send your children to Sunday school and church; take them. Be "the kind of person you want your children and husband to be." "A prudent wife," as the Bible says, "is from the Lord."

RELIGION AND THE CHILDREN

"Train up a child in the way he should go: and when he is old, he will not depart from it." PROV. 22:6

Today we are giving our thought and consideration to the religious care and training of children. Parents, realize that "religion is not so much taught as caught," and that "the parent stands in the place of God" to the child. Then you will see not only the great responsibility that rests upon you, but the sacredness of your task.

The church is a big factor in the training of a child, but it should be considered as a complement to the home. It cannot be a substitute for the parent. The church and the home are two ends of the same thing; their fortunes are inseparable.

But what of the parent who shifts the entire responsibility for the religious training of his child to the church and Sunday school, and that other who seeks to keep his child in religious neutrality until he is able to "choose for himself"? Do such parents think that religion is a foundation put under a house after the house is built? Do they imagine that a life can form habits and consciousness and that that which gives life its significance, depth, height, quality, character, and stability can be added as an appendage?

Religion to be a force in a child's life must begin early in the home. It must be handed down by contagion from parent to child. It must pervade the child's whole being, reactions, attitudes, and feelings about life. Yes, dear parents, the care and religious training of your children is your most important and sacred task. If you fail here, you fail everywhere. It is all very well to talk about the advantages of the church, the power of Truth, etc., "but until the word becomes flesh and dwells in you" who do the talking, your effort is largely in vain. What you give your children by contagion, they will keep and build upon. What you are, they will emulate.

"BE YE THEREFORE IMITATORS OF GOD . . . AND WALK IN LOVE."

THERE IS NOTHING LOST

"There is nothing covered, that shall not be revealed; and hid, that shall not be known." Luke 12:2

To the Mind that knows all, sees all, and hears all, there are no secrets and no losses. The world is full of confused, frustrated, and inattentive people who are always forgetting, losing, or misplacing things. They never seem to know where anything is; and when they want to recall some event, name, or bit of information, they cannot do so. The thing these people need is to realize that the subconscious mind (which is the principal field in which the Holy Spirit works and which is the reservoir of memory) never forgets, misplaces, or loses anything. In fact, all that needs to be done under such circumstances is to establish a reciprocal action between these two minds by calling on the Christ to help them. "Christ in me knows where this thing is (or what I need to know), and He is revealing it to me now. There is nothing lost in Divine Mind, and I am in this Mind now." When this is done, that which is hidden will be revealed. A lost article, name, number, or event will be quickly found.

The first step in synchronizing the conscious and subconscious minds and in strengthening the memory is to give close attention to what you are doing. Memory is one of your most prized possessions. It is not only the source of your identity and conscience, but the measure of your life. It is also the warning factor in your experience. No one is greater than his memory, and no one is less than his memory.

Stimulate your memory into greater action by cultivation, association, repetition, and attention, and by establishing the habit of expecting to remember. When something seems lost or forgotten, do not weaken your memory by disparaging remarks such as "Oh, these memories of ours," but say, "Christ in me never forgets." Then stop all physical and mental activity and call upon Divine Wisdom for what you need to know or find.

"If any man lack wisdom, let him ask of God." Claim the lost thing with deep faith and conviction, saying "There is nothing lost in Divine Mind. The Christ in me knows where this thing is and is revealing it to me now." Then dismiss the loss from your thought and let go. You will be amazed at the results.

BECAUSE I THINK WITH THE MIND OF CHRIST,
I AM BLESSED WITH PERFECT MEMORY.

CHEMISTRY OF THE MIND

"Be ye transformed by the renewing of your mind." Rom. 12:2

This is one of the most concise statements of mental chemistry to be found anywhere in the Bible.

"The key to every man," said Emerson, "is his thought." "Thoughts are things" is the cry of modern metaphysics. "As the lamp to the electric current; as the flame to the fire; as the sunbeam to the sun; as the Word of God to the Spirit of God, so is the body to the mind, and the mind to the Spirit."

When the chemist puts certain chemicals together, he knows precisely what the combination will bring forth. Some will produce clouds of vaporous and colored smoke. Others will produce noxious odors and effervescence; other will explode disastrously.

It is a far cry from chemicals to thoughts; but in a very real sense the mind is a chemist too, producing, by certain combinations of thought, many startling and spectacular results. Some of these results are good; some are bad. Some are exhilarating and satisfying, while others are depressing and terrifying. Some make for heaven; some make for hell. Some make for health; others, for disease. But whether constructive or destructive, thought is the ruling factor in our lives. If we would protect the body, we must protect the mind. If we would renew the body, we must renew the mind. To get the best from the universe, we must think right.

"Have you ever stopped to think how thoughts feel inside your mind? Some are satisfying as bread; some fiery as pepper; some refreshing as water; some heady as wine; some explosive as powder; some nauseating as mustard water. In the mind's storehouse, every thought must be kept sweet and clean if we do not want to breed the gastritis of expression. The most important thing to me is the weather in my mind."

"Choose this day whom ye will serve." Choose whether you will think with the human mind that brings misery, sickness, weakness, worry, and decay, or with the Mind of Christ that brings peace, health, joy, and happiness in God. The source of true thinking is not in books, teachers, or systems of thought, but in God. When the mind is centered in Him, everything falls into its right place.

I NOW SURRENDER MY WHOLE MIND TO GOD,
AND CHRIST CONTROLS MY EVERY THOUGHT.

A NEW CONSCIOUSNESS

"Let this mind be in you, which was also in Christ Jesus." PHIL. 2:5

When we speak of having a Consciousness, we mean a consciousness that is free of self, a consciousness without human limitations. Personal (self) consciousness may be defined as that state of mind which shares its power with evil as well as good, while Spiritual Consciousness is impersonal and knows nothing but Good. It is like the figure of Justice with eye veiled who weighs in the scales in her hands all problems impartially and impersonally. What we call the personal mind is simply our failure to let this Mind which was also in Christ Jesus think through us. It is really unconsciousness, or thinking without God.

In personal consciousness, we share our power with circumstances, conditions, persons, and things. We are subject to all sorts of injuries, injustices, evil opinions, contagion, malicious thoughts, and every form of limitation. In Spiritual Consciousness (consciousness without the knowledge of evil), we are immune to such things. We are immune to them because Light and darkness cannot dwell together. As light always dispels darkness, so the Consciousness of God always dispels the consciousness of self (the human sense of a separate self).

How, then, shall we let this mind be in us which was also in Christ Jesus? How shall we usher in the New Consciousness? By refusing to give power to anything but God, and by giving up the belief that external things can harm or limit us in any way. The New Consciousness does not come into being simply by a change of thoughts in the personal mind, but by our refusal to think with the personal mind or to recognize or to entertain evil suggestions in any form.

The Mind which was also in Christ Jesus is our mind now. It works for us by working through us. It becomes manifest for us to the degree that we give up those things which contradict its fundamental goodness.

> THE MIND OF CHRIST NOW ACTIVE IN MY MIND MAKES ME IMPERSONAL IN ALL MY DEALINGS.

SOME THOUGHTS ON CONSCIOUSNESS

"In Him we live, and move, and have our being." ACTS 17:28

If you will draw a circle on a piece of paper and let it represent the Universe, you will see not only how your consciousness can be expanded in every direction ad infinitum but how everything in that circle will be your consciousness of it.

Then reduce that Universe to its simplest terms and you will say "I AM." In other words, you express consciousness by saying "I AM." Yes, "Life is a state of consciousness," and without consciousness everything would cease to be. Back of and within your consciousness lies practically everything that comprises your life.

Plato, you remember, likened a man's consciousness to a stream that is constantly flowing and changing. "The water [consciousness] changes," he said, "but the river [I AM] remains the same." The problem of controlling consciousness is a problem of keeping it true, accurate, and sound. It is a problem of eliminating the defects and sore spots and of supplanting them with power, beauty, and perfection.

Since consciousness knows nothing but the present moment, we must never permit ourselves to be interested in any other. Jesus said, "Before Abraham was, I Am." If yesterday I was not and tomorrow I shall cease to be, it really makes no difference because today "I Am." That is the only thing that really counts.

The next thing we note about consciousness is that it is impersonal. Like electricity, it will always be to us what we are to it. Having no violation or choice of its own, it will always attract into our lives whatever we set our thought or affection upon.

SUGGESTIONS FOR KEEPING THE CONSCIOUS-
NESS SOUND

1. Discipline your thoughts so that they deal only with the things that are real, permanent, and true. 2. Live, think, and work without fear, worry, resentment, regret, hatred, anxiety, suspicion, bitterness, or criticism. 3. Build a strong faith in God,

and cast upon Him all the problems and difficulties which you cannot solve yourself. 4. Eliminate all superfluous and negative thoughts from your mind, and recreate constantly all affirmatives. 5. Refuse to think about yourself or to feel sorry for yourself. 6. Make no attempt to possess, influence, coerce, or force others to your way of thinking and doing. 7. Cultivate humility, calmness, and patience; always tell the truth. 8. Form no personal or material attachments, but love everybody and everything.

MORE THOUGHTS ON CONSCIOUSNESS

"Be not conformed to this world: but be ye transformed by the renewing of your mind." ROMANS 12:2

Did you every stop to consider why it is that a man who has made a fortune and lost it can make another fortune quicker than the man who has never had one? Or why a certain thing is easy for one man to do and hard for another? Or why everything some men touch turns to gold? Or why a man who has the ability to do difficult things seldom talks about it? Or why one man succeeds m a certain adventure, and another man with equal ability or more favorable endowments fails in the same thing?

Well, it is because these abilities have become second nature (subjective) to the man who succeeds. His consciousness, so to speak, has been turned in the direction of his accomplishment.

Since the basis of all conditions, complexities, circumstances, limitation, Sickness, and trouble is consciousness, and consciousness is the constantly changing factor in our lives, the only way to change conditions is to change our consciousness of them.

If you tell me that you are having a hard time, that nothing goes right with you, that you cannot do a certain thing, then I say, "Look to your consciousness." If you tell me that you cannot get along With the people and that others are always getting in your hair, I say "Like attracts like" and "Like begets like." If you tell me that you never have as much as other people, that your investments always turn out bad, then I say, "Life is a state of consciousness." If you tell me that your health is bad, that your prayers are unanswered, that you get only temporary cures, then I say, "Look to your consciousness."

To get a thing and keep it you must acquire it by right of consciousness.

It you makes no difference, to ·whom you go when trouble— psychologist, psychiatrist, preacher or practitioner—the most that any one can do for you is to help you change your consciousness. If counselors fail here, they fail everywhere. They have nothing more that they can do, and nothing more that they can give.

> THROUGH MY CONSCIOUSNESS OF GOD'S PRESENCE, I CAUSE ALL THINGS TO WORK TOGETHER FOR MY HIGHEST GOOD.

BUILDING A GREATER CONSCIOUSNESS

"Enlarge the borders of your tent." ISAIAH 54:2

The eminent psychologist, William James, said, "Men habitually use only a small part of the powers which they possess." Every one of us has it within ourselves to have more and to be more than we are. Great untouched reservoirs of power lie hidden within us all. We are in touch with

Omnipotence, but we are impotent. We are in touch with genius, but we are mediocre. In a world of plenty, men starve. Instead of enjoying health, prosperity, success, and gladness, countless millions suffer from sickness, poverty, failure, and despair. Why? Because of chaotic, limp, negative, and undisciplined thinking.

We talk much about the need for better conditions, better jobs, and a better world, but what we really need is a technique of creative thinking that will push our consciousness out into the great Infinite Resources that surround us. Where shall we find such a technique? In St. Paul's philosophy of thinking: Philippians 4:8.

Let us begin today to form greater and greater concepts and to demonstrate them in our experience. Let us do this by getting rid of all the thoughts that contract and limit our consciousness and by replacing them with thoughts that expand and release it. Instead. of holding thoughts about our insufficiency, limitations, and restrictions, let us think of the Omnipresent Spirit, Substance, and bounty of God. Let us think of the bigness of the universe the magnitude of the starry heavens, the infinite number of fishes in the seas, the vast expanses of water in the world, the countless grains of sand on the seashores. Let us think of the majesty, grandeur, and wonder of everything God has made until we push our minds out far beyond the range of our present limited concepts.

I NOW CAUSE MY MIND TO EXPAND IN EVERY DIRECTION UNTIL I REALIZE THAT I AM ONE WITH GOD AND ALL HIS BLESSINGS.

SOME THOUGHTS ON MENTAL EQUIVALENTS

"With what measure ye mete, if shall be measured to you again."
MATT. 7:2

A Mental Equivalent is the measure of your belief, or your acceptance of good or evil. It is your conscious comprehension of God's Presence or of His absence. It is the cause of whatever enters your life and whatever leaves your life. The kind of position you have, the kind of friends you make, the kind of home you live in, the kind of opportunities that come to you, the material things you possess, the size of your income, the condition of your health-all are determined by and correspond to specific mental equivalents. Everything in your environment, both desirable and undesirable, is the embodiment of the mental concepts operating through your consciousness. It makes no difference how good or how bad, how large or how small, your mental equivalents are, they are demands upon the Universe which are always met.

It is to your advantage, therefore, to form the kind of mental equivalents you want expressed in your experience and to neutralize those you do not want to materialize. Such an aspiration is perfectly natural and normal, and the possibility of such an accomplishment exist already within the mind of every aspiring soul. Every mind has within itself the power not only to chink away from self, but to think with God in such a way that He will create for him a finer body, greater supply, better conditions, and a perfect environment.

We do not realize our spiritual objectives by trying to crowd or stuff a small mind, but by expanding the consciousness. "We advance only by becoming larger than the place we are filling" and by taking the largest possible view of everything.

THE RULES

The five rules for building and maintaining a new mental equivalent follow: 1. Choose an affirmation which represents the desired changes in your problem. 2. Think on the affirmative side of the problem by keeping your thought changed into it. Think with clear vision and deep interest. Keep your thought serenely confident of the manifestation of the ideal situation you are bringing forth. 3. Have great faith in it and act as though it were already in manifestation. 4. Be certain, expectant, and receptive; do not delay the answer by "looking" for results.

> DAILY HOLD YOUR DESIRE AS AN ALREADY ACCOMPLISHED FACT AND GO ABOUT YOUR BUSINESS WITH JOY AND GLADNESS, WITH PEACE AND QUIET CONFIDENCE; THE LAW IS THEN SURE TO ACT.

THANKSGIVING

"With thanksgiving, let your request be made known unto God."
PHIL 4:6

The surest, simplest, and quickest way to realize God's blessings in your needs and to bring Him into action in your affairs is to form the habit of thanking Him for all things at all times. Thanksgiving combines recognition and realization, praise and blessing. It opens all the faculties to God and creates receptivity in the mind. Thankfulness is not only the open acknowledgment of God's nearness, but an infallible aid in increasing prosperity. It will bring alleviation from suffering of any kind.

Gratitude, as some one has said, is the mother of all virtues. It is also the father (source) of all power. Just as the Lord's Supper (Eucharist) is the central sacrament of our religion, issuing in great gratitude and salvation, so thanksgiving must be the controlling and animating power of our lives. The Great Sacrament of the church is called Eucharist because Eucharist means "thank you." When the Frenchman wishes to express thanks he says, *merci*, the Italian says *gratia*, and the Greek says *eucharisto*.

Carlyle once said that "The wealth of man is the number of things which he loves and blesses and by which he is loved and blessed." Are you a wealthy person? Your wealth depends on how many things you are thankful for. Is there an open circuit between yourself and your spiritual source of supply? Freedom of movement depends upon the depth of your gratitude towards God. Do you realize the best results from your prayers? Your success depends upon your thankfulness and appreciation of what you already have.

"Father, I thank Thee." Take your troubles, problems, and perplexities to God in prayer, and then thank Him for their speedy solution. Thank Him for every blessing, big or small, that comes into your life. Thank Him for your wonderful body and all its functions. Thank Him for your home, your church, your loved ones, your position, your friends, and associates, and all those who serve you. Name the joys, privileges, and opportunities that make your life rich and beautiful, and give thanks for them. Gratitude, like all other spiritual principles, is cumulative in its effect. The more you practice it, the more you increase your good.

GRATEFULLY I GIVE THANKS TO GOD FOR ALL MY BLESSINGS.

THERE IS MORE OF YOU

"[God] is able to do for us exceeding abundantly above all that we ask or think, according to the power that worketh in us." Eph. 3:20

In these days when we are tempted to think of ourselves as powerless against the mighty tides of evil that threaten us, we need to think of the Source of All Power, which is God. We need to make an honest appraisal of our own ills, problems, and limitations and to admit that they are result of living and thinking without God — the effect of our failure to put Him first in all things.

We need to keep in mind the words of St. Paul: "Power belongeth unto God." It belongs to God because there are two ways of using it. The power of good is also the power of evil "The very power that can and will save us, becomes the power that can and will destroy us if it used unwisely."

"Hear, O, Israel, the Lord our God is One. That is the first step in using power wisely. "Acknowledge me in all thy ways." That is the second step. Acknowledge that all the power you have is part of the One Power and that it will always be to you what you are to It and your sense of futility will be replaced by confidence.

You can increase this power in your life by thinking, working, and living in the knowledge that there is more of you than appears on the surface. Know that deep down in your being there is a Power so immense that no limit or measure can ever be placed upon it. Trust It to unlock the door to everything that is desirable and wonderful in yourself. Contemplate It until It changes everything in your life. Available is more of me, more of you, more of everything. Act It out. Live It. Believe It. Be It, and It will come forth.

"The word of God is instant and powerful and it *always* works." Know this truth so thoroughly that it supplants every opposing belief in your mind: I have the power! more power than I know — full power! All the power hat God has is mine — God Power. All the God — power I can perceive, accept, and use. The power to bless, to remedy, to heal — I have that power. The power to know, and know and know, until the glad blessings I have evoked from God's invisible real shall come out forth God's invisible realm shall come forth into full, splendid, unadulterated fruition — I have that Power.

THE WORD OF GOD IS INSTANT AND POWERFUL, AND IT ALWAYS WORKS.

WHERE MOST STUDENTS FAIL.

". . . for be endured, as seeing him who is invisible." HEB. 11:27

Probably the most difficult step in metaphysical science is to make the transition from the visible to the invisible, from matter to Spirit, from effect to cause. Having relied for the greater part of our lives upon material means and human agencies, we do not find it easy suddenly to shift the center of gravity from the seen to the unseen. We are so used to working with the tangible and ponderable things of life that the invisible things seem inconsequential. Although the greater part of our activity is in the realm of the tangible, we know that every act we perform is prefaced by a thought.

The word *metaphysics* means above form; not until we can think and work from this basis can we gain dominion over our world. When we write a letter, or dial a number on the telephone, water the lawn, or bake a cake, we are aware that something very definite is being done. When we carry on a conversation with a friend, we know by his reaction what effect our words have had. All this is changed, however, when it comes to treating ourselves or others, for here we work with things that cannot be seen, heard, touched, or felt. Here we must trust where we cannot see, and must believe where we cannot hear. It is not easy to realize that our word has power or that we are accomplishing anything through our prayers, unless we know that it is the Universal and not the individual mind that we are calling into action in our lives. Jesus said, "It is the Father within that doeth the work." The power which the metaphysician invokes is spiritual, not material; subjective, not objective.

God requires of us just two things—surrender and trust; we must give ourselves and all our interests into His care and keeping. What is so difficult about that? Why do we make it so hard? It should be as easy to give ourselves and our interests to God as it is to give Him the responsibility for digesting our food or for developing the seed which we plant in the ground. Let us begin to apply this principle today by leaving everything quietly to God. Trusting God is the secret of peace, efficiency, power, and achievement.

> I WILLINGLY SURRENDER MYSELF AND ALL MY INTERESTS TO GOD, IN ORDER THAT MY CHRIST SELF MAY BE EXPRESSED.

THE LAW OF GOOD

"And God saw everything He had made, and, behold, it was very good." GEN. 1:31

The first thing a man does when harnessing the principle of electricity to his individual needs is to obey the laws of electricity. The first thing he does when applying the Truth to his many problems is to obey the Law of God. Obedience is the lever which sets the law m operation. Just as electricity is everywhere equally present but "shines forth," or "becomes" self-conscious, in the bulb," God who Is Omnipresent becomes self-conscious in man. Man does not approach Principle but specializes It through his mind, his word, and his obedience to the Law. In metaphysics, the Principle, or Fact is our only rule of demonstration.

"And God saw everything he had made and, behold, it was very good." The Kingdom of Heaven is finished. "God's work is done. He is the Law. He is the supply. Our work is to obey the Law, to receive and distribute the supply." A common failing of beginners Truth is an attempt to use the Law without conforming to its terms. That is, they try to use it without meeting the conditions laid down for its operation.

Over and over again, Jesus put these conditions into words: Go all the way with the Law. Go. the Second Mile. Go seventy times seven. Give your cloak with your coat. Turn the other cheek. Love God with all your heart, soul, strength, and mind. Love your neighbor as yourself. Know the Truth that nothing unlike God can operate in your life. If God is All and He is One, then there is nothing but God.

Webster defines Principle or Law as "a set rule of perfect action." Law is not. a person with powers of choice; law has no choice but to obey its own terms. If the conditions are met, that is if our minds are centered in the affirmative side of good, the Law will work for us. If they are not met, It will work against us. But whether for or against, the Principle is both Cause and Effect. "Whatsoever a man soweth, that shall he also reap."

Let us begin to apply this Law of Good by knowing that the Goodness of God, inherent within us, comes forth as that very good we desire.

GOD, THE LAW OF GOOD, IS THE ONLY LAW OPERATING IN MY LIFE.

"ALL THINGS WORK TOGETHER . . . "

Read: Gen. 50:14-20.

"All things work together for good to them that love God." ROM. 8:28

Joseph, now a mighty man in Egypt, forgot the treatment and injury of his brothers in the consciousness that there was a Divine plan running through his life. "Ye thought evil against me; but God meant it unto good."

Now, analyze that statement and you will find that it is one of the greatest weapons against innuendoes, criticism, affronts, and hurts to be found anywhere. To impute evil to those who are mean, unlovely, sarcastic, and antagonistic is very easy. To see the worst that is in them and to build up an unsympathetic feeling against them is easy. But to love those same people, to see the good that is in them and to call it forth, is another thing altogether.

In all the Bible there is no more glorious promise of a principle fulfilled than in the eighth chapter of St. Paul's epistle to the Romans: "For we know that all things work together for good to them that love God." Now let us analyze this statement step by step.

WE KNOW THAT ALL THINGS . . . That is an all-inclusive and sweeping statement. Not something apart from other things. Not some things easy to heal and demonstrate over. Not many things or most things, but all things—hard things, impossible things, incurable things, disappointing things, ugly things.

WORK TOGETHER . . . When our thoughts are centered in God, we bring the Power of the Infinite into expression. God then works on our behalf. Whatever is lacking will be supplied. Whatever is weak will be strengthened. Whatever is sick will be healed.

FOR GOOD . . . Not always the way we want them. Not always the way we think they ought to be. But always for our highest good.

TO THEM THAT LOVE GOD . . . This is the greatest point of all. Things do not work together for good to just anybody and everybody—but to those who "love God;" that is, to those who enter into and share His. quality of consciousness.

> GOD'S LOVE NOW EXPRESSED IN ME CAUSES ALL THINGS TO WORK TOGETHER FOR MY HIGHEST GOOD.

SUPPLY AND DEMAND

"And my God shall supply all your need according to His riches in glory by Christ Jesus." PHIL. 4:19

One of the first steps in demonstrating supply of any kind is the realization that the law of supply and demand is always equal. Since God is Omnipresent (everywhere equally present), wherever there is need there is complete, instant, and Self-Operative supply. When Jesus called attention to "the lilies of the field, how they grow," He was pointing out the law of nature which is always operative. Just as the demands of growing plants are met by keeping the seeds and bulbs in perfect contact with the elements and forces of Nature, the demands of man are supplied when his mind is kept in perfect contact with God.

Study a weather map and the movement of the air between high and low pressure areas, and you will see how this law works and how Nature seeks always to maintain a balance. "A low pressure area indicates a lack of normal quantity or density of air. This low pressure necessitates a corresponding high pressure area at some other point." In other words, supply and demand are in direct ratio to each other.

"When the demand develops simultaneously and the weather forecaster identifies a low-pressure area, he begins at once to locate the high-pressure area which he knows must exist. When these two points, the high and the low pressure areas, are located, he can then determine in which direction the next movement of the air will be. That movement will be from the high which is a superabundance of air, toward the low, where it is lacking. From these facts, the direction of the wind is determined." The movement must originate in THAT WHICH HAS and proceed to that which has not. The wind does not cease its movement until the demand is supplied.

If you will now think of the negative—ignorance, disease, poverty, separation, etc.—as the low pressures in your lives, you will see how, when you open yourself to the Divine Presence, God moves in to counteract them.

CENTERED IN GOD, I KNOW MY SUPPLY IS ASSURED.

DEMONSTRATING PROSPERITY

"Whosoever hath, to him shall be given." LUKE 8:18

Since poverty and prosperity are both the outpicturing of states of mind, one is just as much a demonstration as the other. Increase and decrease, expansion and contraction are the re-suits of the operation of a Universal Law. Both are ideas in consciousness, and both manifest according to the power and prominence given them in our thought. "I have set before you life and death, blessing and cursing; choose ye." If the idea of poverty is allowed to rule in consciousness, we get stagnation, disintegration, and deterioration on the outer plane. If the idea of prosperity rules, we get circulation, activity, and riches.

There is but One Substance in the Universe out of which all things are made, people, houses, automobiles, aeroplanes, trains, ships, dogs, money, food, clothing, and skyscrapers. This is the reason why "thoughts are things" and why a man becomes what he thinks. God Substance, which is omnipresent and inexhaustible, stands under all matter and form. It is that element out of which we are created, in which we live, move and have our being, and by which we arc fed, healed, sustained, and prospered. God Substance is not affected by man's fear, or talk of hard times because it is never depleted.

The first thing to do when finances run low, then is to reverse the polarity of your thought and faith, and to realize your unity with the "One living Substance which is God" and your sufficiency in all things. In other words, seek the consciousness of Substance and not money. Money is a dead symbol. It has no intelligence or life because God is the only Intelligence and Life there is. To pray or treat for money is never legal, wise, or scientific.

"Whosoever hath, to him shall be given." Since substance is with us always and "is first given form in the mind," what we need at such a time is to provide larger channels for its expression. How shall we do that? By keeping the mind filled with Universal Substance and by working in harmony with God's Law of supply. Our part is to keep our minds centered in God and free from negative thoughts of financial limitation; His part is to give us all that we need.

THE INVISIBLE SUBSTANCE IS PLASTIC TO MY ABUNDANT THOUGHT AND I AM RICH IN MIND AND IN MANIFESTATION.

STIR UP THE GIFT

The difference between poverty and prosperity is in the rate of vibration. The rich man vibrates at one rate, while the poor man vibrates at another. The healthy man, at one rate; the sick man, at another. Happy people, at one rate; despondent people, at another. Positive people, at one rate; negative people, at another. There are more poor people in the world than rich ones because every rate of vibration operates on its own plane of activity. It never mixes with its opposite on another plane.

"Did you ever see mud stay up in the air? Well, the same thing applies to these invisible environments. The faster a thing vibrates, the higher it climbs. The slower it vibrates, the lower it sinks. It is these different rates of vibration which constitute man's environment."

Poverty is the outpicturing of a demagnetized state of mind. The poor man stagnates because he lacks the magnetism which is needed to attract success.

We are recommending in today's lesson that everyone seeking to demonstrate prosperity begin now to raise his rate of vibration. You can do this in three ways: By changing your thoughts, your feelings, and your surroundings. If you have been thinking and talking limitation, poverty, economy, failure, trouble, and discouragement, clear your mind of all this rubbish. Determine to keep all your old pessimistic and troublesome thoughts locked up for one week. See yourself as prosperous: talk and act as though you were.

Do not desire prosperity, but BE IT. Desire is an admission of lack. Reverse it by saying with deep conviction and acceptance, "I AM PROSPERITY." Then see it as a reality. If you have been feeling low and depressed, start your day with vigorous exercise, sending your affirmation, "I AM PROSPERITY" tingling through your whole body.

Now, stir things up in your home and office. Change things around. Move the furniture into new positions. Clean out your bill fold, files, and drawers. Discard everything that is not serving some useful purpose. Send all soiled things to the cleaners. Paint the wood work. Make the floor shine. Surround yourself with beauty, color, and freshness. This will help lift you to a more magnetic plane of thought and action.

Repeat until it forms in you a consciousness of itself:

"I AM PROSPERITY."

KEYS TO PROSPERITY

"Thou shalt decree a thing, and it shall be established unto thee."
JOB 22:28

1. Consciously or unconsciously, we are always decreeing something. It is a wise man, therefore, who thinks thoughts and speaks words that increase his supply instead of decreasing it.

2. To make your prosperity permanent and enduring, realize your oneness with God Substance from which all your good comes.

3. In demonstrating prosperity, do not think about yourself, your needs, your obligation, or your limitations, but realize the Presence of God and the nature of Universal Substance. Bless your purse, your blank account, and your business, and see them filled with living substance ready to take form.

4. Open the way for prosperity by blessing everything you now have. Speak words of blessing over present possessions, and they will increase and multiply. Know that your words are spirit, that they are life, and that they accomplish that whereunto they are sent.

5. When working for a larger income, never permit yourself to see lack in anything or anybody. Do not criticize, scold, or find fault and do not belittle yourself. If you say, "I am hard up, poor, or out of cash," you are placing a limit on the Substance in your mind. You are repelling your good instead of attracting it.

6. Keep dynamic prosperity statements coursing through your mind constantly. The more you present these truths to the inner mind, the stronger your conviction becomes.

7. Since "increase comes by the operation of a Universal Law," never take personal credit for what comes to you or for what you make. Praise God instead of self.

8. Eliminate all negative and poverty-stricken thoughts from your mind. Talk prosperity, live prosperity, think prosperity, and give thanks for prosperity.

9. Never depend upon salary, bank account, or investments, but upon God. Know that He is your only Employer and that He gives you your right recompense.

10. Practice the Law of Non-Possession by knowing that you are a channel and not a terminal. Since everything belongs to God and returns to God, you are only a steward over material possessions. They are yours to use but not to keep.

11. Be a good steward. Keep your affairs in contact with Creative Activity by returning one-tenth of your income to Its Source. You can do this by tithing to the church or to any organization from which you receive your spiritual help. It is the Law of sowing and reaping.

12. Be thankful. Thank God for the fulfillment of your desires before and after they are manifested. The more thankful you are for what comes to you, the more you will receive.

FILL IT UP

"Heaven and earth are full of Thee."

Here is one of the best ways to keep your mind filled with the inexhaustible God-Substance: Remove from your environment everything that suggests poverty or reacts upon you in the way of detraction "and keep everything around you filled to the brim."

If you have allowed things to run down and empty out, refill them. Show your utter contempt for poverty by changing your thoughts, your attitudes, your habits, and your personal appearance. Remove all the things from your · person and your surroundings that suggest lack. Change your feelings by changing your looks, and the looks of things.

If you have allowed your shoes to run down at the heel, have them repaired or replace them by new ones. If socks are over-darned or underwear ragged, get new. Keep plenty of fresh linen on hand. "Heaven and earth are full of Thee." See that your clothes are always clean and pressed; get a new suit if you need one, and trust God to pay for it. Clothes will not make you, but they will help to discover you. In other words, get into the atmosphere of prosperity. Radiate it. Claim it as your own. Study prosperous people, their ways, and the luxury that surrounds them; "then imagine yourself in their places."

Look for the best, and buy the best. Keep your standards high and the Law will attract to you those things which are like your thoughts. This is a principle; it applies to all things. Keep your fountain pen filled. Keep on hand a plentiful supply of soap, blades, shaving cream and tooth paste, and do not pinch the tubes until dry. Fill the coal bin to overflowing; keep the sugar bowl filled. Trim the yard regularly; do not allow the house to run down and become shoddy-looking. Keep your gas tank filled and avoid the risk of being stalled; keep your windshield clean so you can look out upon a clear track and "see the fullness of God." In fact, do everything that will generate prosperity vibrations.

Help everyone that comes to your door, even if only with a kindly, positive, and helpful word. In fact, do everything on the outside that will carry out the feeling of affluence and power.

"Thoughts are things." "As a man thinketh in his heart so is he." Keep your mind alive toward your goal by feeding it with prosperity ideas. "Heaven and earth are full of Thee."

HOW IS YOUR SPIRIT?

"Not by might, nor by power, but by spirit, saith the Lord of Hosts." ZECH. 4:6

"Where there is no spirit, the people perish. Where there is no spirit, the nations perish. Where there is no spirit, the churches perish. The word without the spirit is dead."

The body without the spirit is dead. Prayer without the spirit is dead. Faith without the spirit is dead. Love without the spirit is dead. Anything without the spirit is dead. It 1s the Spirit that giveth life.

A man may possess light bulbs and have his house wired, but without electricity he cannot have light. With electricity coming through the proper channel, he may have illumination whenever he chooses. It is so with the body and the spirit. A man may talk glibly of subduing the flesh and letting in the Spirit, but that is like saying that electric light bulbs will give light without connection with the power plant. The one without the other is dead.

It makes no difference what you call this energizing, life—giving agent-mind, consciousness, principle, or spirit. It is that by which you live, think, act, move, and work, and by which you succeed or fail. "There is a spirit in man"—in every man, and the condition of his spirit is up to him. And what is this spirit? It is our point of contact with God, the unseen, the animating part of our being, which makes us what we are.

"It is the spirit that giveth life." The spirit gives life, quality, caliber, and character to everything that we think, say, feel, or do. It gives tone to our whole being and to our every experience. It affects every thought we think, every belief we entertain, and every emotion we foster. If our spirit is weak, sick, frustrated, distorted, drooping, ugly, timid or fearful, it must be made over, altered, restored.

How does one accomplish this? By cultivating new psychological and mental habits, by decentralizing the self, and by loyal cooperation with God. Then no longer shall we be identified with limitation, failure, friction, inertia, and worry, but we shall manifest plenty, success, harmony, vitality, and confidence.

"The Spirit beareth witness with our spirit, chat we are the children of God." When we are centered in Christ Consciousness, God's Spirit and our spirit come together so that nothing foreign or inimical can exist between them.

> I AM FREE. NOTHING IN THE WORLD HAS THE POWER TO BIND MY SPIRIT.

"MOSQUITOES CAN'T STING ELEPHANTS."

" . . . what is that to thee? Follow thou me." JOHN 21:22

Preventing outer conditions and influences, from disturbing you can be likened to cleaning tar from your shoes. The tar first smears the stick and paper you use for a wiper, then your fingers, your clothes and eventually, almost everything within reach.

So many things disturb us; people upset us, irritations beset us, situations hurt our feelings, conditions influence us unfavorably, countless things make us angry, unhappy, or fearful.

Why is this? We permit the lower to affect the higher, the outer to affect the Inner. St. Paul asked: "Who did hinder you that ye should not obey the Truth?" Jesus said: "Come apart from among them, and be ye separate." There is the remedy — the only way you can get the grade of stability that outer influences cannot upset.

The commission has already been given: "Let them have dominion over all the earth." You have dominion! You have authority! You have power! What keeps you subdued and insecure? You have surrendered your passivity; you have allowed people and conditions, instead of God, to control your thoughts. What you need is not resistance and pugnacity but passivity and detachment. You need to learn how to let go and to think of your problem only objectively. You need a "relaxed musculature" and a quiet mind. You need to spend more time in bringing out the Christ and less time in reacting to the world.

In your experiences do you encounter adversaries? If they master you, you have lost dominion. Jesus said: "Agree with thine adversary quickly." In other words, turn your thoughts from self to God. Expand your consciousness of God's Presence so that the claims of the outer world can find nothing in you with which to work. That is what we mean by "Mosquitoes can't sting elephants." If you would save wear and tear on heart, stomach, and nerves, practice passivity of thought.

MY CONSCIOUSNESS OF GOD'S PRESENCE "CAUSES ME TO SEE ALL SITUATIONS FROM THE STANDPOINT OF TRUTH."

"EVERYTHING HAPPENS TO ME."

"And we know that all things work together for good to them that love God." ROM. 8:28

A friend relates this experience: "While. descending a precipitous mountain road, my right front tire blew out. It could hardly have happened in a more inconvenient or more dangerous place, and the words I uttered characterized the gone feeling I felt within myself: 'Everything happens to me.'

"It was a hot day and I was hurrying to reach a hotel before darkness. Not only the irritating delay of tire-changing was in prospect, but when I opened my trunk I found that the spare tire also was flat. 'Everything happens to me!'

"Then I realized, as I again was speeding over the highway, how futile and pathetic my irritation. has been. No misfortune had really happened. Neither my vacation nor my life had come suddenly to an end. MY car had not gone over the mountain and been destroyed. No one had been hurt. Suddenly, it was an occasion for praise and thanksgiving!"

What the Apostle is trying to show us in our text is that the quickest, most effective way to meet whatever happens to us is not by holding an attitude of impatience, self-pity, negativeness, or pessimism but by acknowledging the Presence of the Spirit of Christ.

The important thing in trying situations is always our reaction to them. If there is an outburst at such times, the thought back of our words is muddled when it should be clear, poised, life-giving, and constructive. It may bring temporary relief to wail, "Everything happens to me," but such a statement only lays the foundation for more trouble.

We should never give expression to that which we do not wish to experience. Instead of thinking of ourselves as victims of calamity, we should know that we are more than conquerers through Him Who loves us and who gave Himself for us.

THE LOVE OF CHRIST IN THE MIDST OF ME EVER GIVES ME DOMINION AND AUTHORITY OVER EVERY SITUATION IN MY WORLD.

SOME THOUGHTS ON CHANGING CONDITIONS

1. If you do not wish to remain where conditions are bad, stop complaining about them Stop resisting them. The quickest way to overcome unfavorable circumstances is to practice non-resistance and non-recognition. When you contend with circumstances or condition, you only prolong their existence.
2. To turn adversaries into blessings, you must meet them in an attitude of perfect harmony. Changing conditions does not depend alone upon one's education, mental acumen, or spirituality. It is not a question of hard work, evolution, or strife. It is not brought about by the use of will power, vehement denial, or vigorous affirmation. It depends upon maintaining absolute stillness.
3. When you develop fineness, quality, and spirituality within yourself (just by being what you are), you will meet all conditions. You will attract conditions, associations, and friends which are after your own heart.
4. If you want God's Law of Good to rule in your life you must embody that idea in your thought. Declare that it is so. Involve it in your mind. Know that your mind

receives it. Know that your mind believes it. Know that your mid accepts it. Know that your mind acts upon it. Know that your mind produces with it.

5. Work daily to bring yourself to that place in consciousness where there are no mistakes, no failures, no misunderstandings, and no misfortunes; where there is nothing but peace, poise, power, plenty, health, happiness, and wholeness.

6. When working to make a demonstration, know that your word is the one thing you seek to realize. See your desire as already fulfilled; then dismiss it from your mind. Be confident and certain; do not strain for results or allow yourself to worry, to be hurried or anxious.

7. When things go wrong, declare that they have no power over you. "No mistakes have been made, none is being made, and none can be made." Then clear your mind by repeating: "There is One Supreme Intelligence which governs, guides, and guards, tells me what to do, when to act, and how to act. I now act with perfect assurance."

8. The way to control condition is to control self — to bring yourself to the place in consciousness where conditions no longer have the power over you. Reality appears when you perceive the nothingness of illusion. Right in the midst of your most serious illness is perfect health. In the midst of your greatest problem is that problem's answer. When you wish peace, you do not have to drive discord from your mind and body you simply change your consciousness and become aware of peace.

9. "Acknowledge me in al thy ways, and I will give thee the desires of thy heart." God does not expect us to create health, supply, and other blessings of ourselves, but only to acknowledge their existence. He does not

ask us to destroy disease, inharmony, and imperfection, but only to recognize that "Nothing shall by any means hurt you." He does not ask us to deny the existence of evil but to perceive the good, to dwell upon it, and to expect it.

A PARADOX

"For unto everyone that hath shall be given, and he shall have abundance: but from him that hath not shall be taken away even that which he hath." MATT. 25:29

This is one of those rare declarations of Jesus which impress us at first as being paradoxical. Why not give to the man that has not and let the other man be content with what he has? But, though that may sound logical, it is not a true report of life as it is; whereas Jesus' statement, whether we like it or not, is accurate.

He who is conscious of much shall receive more; he who is conscious of little shall lose that which he has. Why is this so? The basis of all attraction and possession is consciousness, and not outward circumstances or conditions. If a man's consciousness of accumulation is rightly directed (toward God and Heaven), he will attract tangible possessions. If he lacks such consciousness, he will not only lose that which he does possess, but he shall shut out the better things from his life.

Now, let us think of two men seemingly of equal ability and endowments. We will call the first man A and the second man B. A is a tireless worker, capable, sincere, educated, and of good character. But he never gets ahead. He receives a meager salary, and his affairs always are in reverse. He does not hold what he gets; the good things seem to fall away from him. He is a failure.

B, on the other hand, with less education and natural ability, has good things in abundance. He does not need to seek opportunities; they seek him. He has plenty of money, good times, clothes, automobiles, and a beautiful home. His investments pay large dividends; he sells merchandise when there appears to be no market. He attracts the best from everybody and everything. In many ways, B seems inferior to A; but A fails while B succeeds.

In what way do these two men differ? Is It in education, ability, industry, or personality? No, it is in consciousness. B, while lacking many of the finer qualities, is positive toward his good. He consciously visualizes that which he wishes to attain, and this condition of mind acts as a magnet which draws tangible blessings generous measure to him. A n the other hand, is negative an unseeing; he repels good. His restricted consciousness prevents t e good getting into his life.

Thus to "Everyone that hath shall be given: but from him that hath not, shall be taken away even that which he hath."

THE LAW OF GOOD IS THE ONLY LAW AT WORK IN MY LIFE.

"I SING FOR GOD"

"Whether therefore ye eat, or drink, or whatsoever ye do, do all to the glory of God." I Cor. 10:32

Few realize the great benefits to be "derived from thinking, working, and living to the glory of God. A dancer was failing in her work when her director, a metaphysical student, suggested that she start dancing to the glory of God. She had done poorly in rehearsals and unless she got into the spirit of her work, he would not be able to keep her in the ballet. She had a mother to support and needed the money. The young woman prayed; then she acted upon the director's advice. Now she is one of America's most famous and highly paid dancers.

Jenny Lind summed up the great purpose of her life in four words: "I sing for God." The shepherds, going back to their tasks each held his secret in his own heart, saying to himself, "I keep sheep for God." The Wise Men said, "WE study the stars for God." We can say: "I drive an automobile for God," "I keep books for God," I build bridges for God," "I do housework for God," "I practice medicine for God," "I nurse the sick for God," "I mend shoes for God," "I make money for God." "Glory to God in the highest!"

It makes no difference what your job or profession may be, you will always do it better and receive a greater return if you do it to the glory of God, if you think of Him and not man as your employer. "Whether, therefore ye eat, or drink, or whatsoever ye do, do all to the glory of God."

In other words, integrate your work and activities with God. Take Him with you wherever you go and into everything you do. See Him in the commonplace as well as in the miraculous. "See every common bush afire with God."

If a task seems hard, take God with you, and He will perform it through you. Do not depend upon your own puny power; use your power plus God's Power. Do not see your limitations, problems, troubles, fears, and worries, but His ever-present

Life, Wisdom, and Love. "For thine is the Kingdom, and the Power, and the Glory forever."

When you take God with you, you take that which knows no defeat.

I SUCCEED IN EVERYTHING I UNDER TAKE BECAUSE I DO ALL TO THE GLORY OF GOD.

THE FATHER'S BUSINESS

"Wist ye not that I must be about my Father's business?" ST. LUKE 2:49

Our lesson today is on Divine cooperation. When Jesus' parents found Him in the temple, He was surprised that they had not looked there first. We do not know what He thought to be His Father's business, but we may be sure that it was not something foreign to His daily life, to the carpenter shop, or to His home. It was not something that was confined to the Sabbath, special days, or sacred places; but it was intimately associated with everything secular.

Just as there are some who confine their patriotism to the Fourth of July, there are those who keep their religion for church, Sundays, and holy days. They are religious in a churchly sort of way, but they do not see religion in its relation to daily life. It does nothing for them because they do not use it. They think of it more as a Sunday dinner than daily bread, more as an escape from misery than a way to happiness. They think of it as something to die by, rather than to live by.

St. Paul said: "Whether, therefore, ye eat, or drink, or whatsoever ye do, do all to the glory of God." Whatever our tasks may be, we should perform them in the right spirit, to His glory. It is God's Will that the right principle be used daily in whatever we do.

The Father works according to Principle, and our part is to let the Principle work through us. How? By removing all doubt from our minds and by thinking positively toward God. God works with us as we work with Him.

COOPERATING WITH GOD, I FIND DIVINE COOPERATION WHEREVER I GO.

"IT IS FINISHED."

It was a Persian philosopher who said: "That which ought to be is; therefore, let us rest."

That which is and ought to be IS NOW. "That which is, and ought to be, is GOOD." That which is, and ought to be, is perfect. That which is, and ought to be, is God, infinite, changeless, and enduring. There are not two creations—the one material and the other spiritual. There is only ONE, and it is finished.

There are not two powers, one evil and the other good. There is only one: GOD IS GOOD. That which seems to be material and that which seems to be evil are nothing more than your own states of mind which are out of adjustment with the Divine. plan. You do not see it as it is.

How strange that it should take the followers of Christ 2000 years to discover that the Kingdom of Heaven is not a place to be attained through suffering, death, struggle, hard work, and arduous thinking, but an ideal state of mind already perfected by Christ and only awaiting our recognition of it and experience of it! Indeed, contemporary religion and metaphysics remind one of the mazes of the seventeenth century built in gardens to confuse trespassers. A maze is a confusing network of meandering paths which lead nowhere. We build our mazes by trying to demonstrate things instead of letting them come to us. "Use this technique," says one. "Breathe this way," says another. "Avoid starches," says someone else. Follow the stars! Study the Pyramids! Gaze into a crystal! Go to this fortune teller! Study Spiritualism! Jesus said, "Follow me." "No man cometh unto the Father, but by me." St. Paul said, "Let this Mind be in you, which was also in Christ Jesus."

Spiritual demonstration is not a matter of getting something from the outside, but a matter releasing something which is already have, and then being that thing. When are you going to stop studying history and begin to make it? When are you going to stop reading Truth and begin to use it? When are you going to exchange your coming Kingdom for a present Kingdom and begin to live in it?

Are you going to wait another 2000 years? Well, take as long as you wish. But, remember, appropriation begins when you "give thanks"; yes, even before there is any visible signs of the thing you are seeking, or before you have had time to shape your wish into words.

If you are serious about finding your good, say every time your need comes to mind:

"IT IS FINISHED!" "IT IS DONE."

Then have done with it and REST.

Note on Robert A Russell: RobertARussell.Org

I have spent the last 5 years tracking down the works of this exceptional mystic and I believe I have found approximately 95% of his lost works. I am constantly on the search for his lost titles, here is a list of our current titles:

GOD Works Through Faith
GOD Works Through You
GOD Works Through Silence
All Things Made New
Dry Those Tears
I Have Found the Way
Getting Better Results from Spiritual Practice
In Spite of Everything
Making the Contact
Quickest Way to Everything Good
Talk Yourself Out of It
Talk Yourself Into It
The Laboratory of Silence
This Works
Victory Over Fear and Worry
Vital Points in Demonstration
You Can Get What You Want
You Too Can Be Prosperous
You Try It
The Answer Will Come

If you are currently living in Colorado, or have a family member or know anyone that has anymore of his works and want to h elp us continue his spiritual legacy, please drop us an email to aepublish@gmail.com

We would be happy to purchase your books.
Thank you, Barry Peterson, Publisher

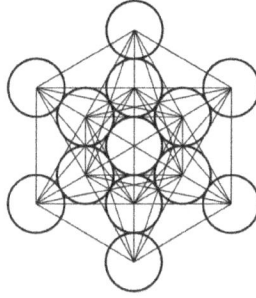

Raisa - Mystic Alchemist

Energy Healing, Chakra Alignment, Sacred Geometry, Sound Healing

Tammy:

I was blessed with a healing session by Raisa last week. She felt like a friend and like-minded gentle soul with comforting Mother Mary essence pouring through her words. Raisa was so in-tuned to my blocks and traumas held within my field. She used her connection to ascended masters I've resonated with such as Yeshua, Mother Mary, Mary Magdalene, Lady Vesta & Amethyst and archangels Metatron, Michael and others to help clear these.

I was able to address childhood trauma situations to flip the stuck energy I've held onto over the years. She also picked up on a few traumatic past-life scenes that have affected my current life. I am an intuitive energy healer who truly felt the shift and healing within. I now feel so much lighter and have clarity regarding my path.

So much love and gratitude to you both, Raisa and Barry for presenting her to my world! (More Testimonials on following Pages)

Contact Raisa to book an Energy Healing
or Chakra Alignment session:
www.RaisinYourIsness.com
raisinyourisness@hotmail.com

Shannon:
This BEAUTIFUL sister...our Raisa... is a treasure beyond compare! After my experience in my personal session with Raisa... the ABSOLUTE confirmation I received, that could ONLY be confirmed by HER mind you... this session solidified EVERYTHING for me. I KNOW that this sister... she is a formidable, magnificent & IRREPLACEABLE component in this Earth plane story we all are invested in! IF YOU ARE DRAWN TO HER FOLLOW YOUR HEART

No other can do what SHE is gifted to do for YOU... YES YOU!

I LOVE YOU dear sister! I am forever grateful for what only you could do and DID for me! I would have happily paid any price for what you gave me! I URGE YOU ALL to schedule a session with this beloved one!

P.S. thank you Barry for sharing her with us all!

∞

Natasha:
I would like to thank Barry for introducing us to Raisa. I have had 2 consultations with her in the last month and I am in total awe of what transpired. Raisa is such a beautiful caring soul! She connected with me as though she has known me forever. Her love and dedication in assisting others is so touching. I had an amazing experience and some profound healing. I received a message from Jeshua which brought tears to my eyes. I could feel the LOVE in the message that was given to me and I will remember and cherish His message forever. Raisa has really helped me in confronting fears, trauma and past life karma. I have found the reason for my skin problems which I never would have thought it'd be possible. It is amazing what guilt and shame from past lives can actually do to your body. Her healing and that from our Angelic beings has really made a huge difference in my life. I can feel it in my energy. Raisa has a lovely sense of humour, always reminding you not to take life and yourself so seriously. I really feel like a heavy weight has been lifted off my soul. Thank you so much! Much Love!

∞

Ariel:

Raisa... Divine Raisa... You are a Treasure to this Life, and I thank All That Is, and this also Treasured YT channel for the priceless blessing which was our session this AM. Every moment of the session was a fractal explosion of wonderful intuitive & divinely guided perfection. I honor your sincere, caring, graceful, playful, soothing, encouraging, transformational, empowering, and so beautiful demonstration / embodiment of Goddess energy and presence. I am so honored & thankful to have been guided to You. To have invested in the patience, time, energy, and resources to share sacred healing and uplifting time with You. I will remember the session Always. And I will look forward to any and all ways our Creator deems it harmonious to connect again. I could go on and on and on, so please accept my parting acknowledgment of your blessing to this realm, my Heart & Spirt, my Life, and the Lives of all those who may be positively impacted via your assistance. Blessings, and Gratitude, a thousand times over and over again. Namaste... Namaste... Namaste...

∞

B.G.

I have just finished a healing session with Raisa. The experience was remarkable! I am still buzzing! I heard about her from this channel, so thank you deeply Barry!

Raisa is so lovely to talk to, and intuitively guided, knows how to get to the hidden roots of our issues. She calls upon ascended masters, archangels and such to do deep energetic clearing and healing work. It was like being guided through the deep layers of myself, releasing the things that don't serve me and filling every cell with light. I purged, and I absorbed new energy, and came out feeling uplifted and renewed. Raisa helped me to find things in myself that I had been cut off from, and to heal wounds I had tried to bury. She has also given me helpful ideas to continue to improve things my life.

I am so blessed to have found Raisa, and ever grateful for the healing work she has done. She is as authentic as they come. Truly an earth angel! Thank you, thank you, thank you!

▶ YouTube

YouTube Channels of Interest:

Giving Voice to the Wisdom of the Ages

Over 5,000 audios, hundreds of
Spiritual and Metaphysical
audio books including
Robert A Russell, Dr Murdo MacDonald Bayne,
Napoleon Hill, Jeshua, Kryon and many more.

I AM Meditations and Affirmations

Hundreds of I AM Meditations,
Daily affirmations and more.

Raisin' Your Isness

Metaphysical Musings, Channelings,
Sound Healing Songs

www.ingramcontent.com/pod-product-compliance
Lightning Source LLC
Chambersburg PA
CBHW031259090426
42742CB00007B/517